THE JAPAN-U.S.
ASSEMBLY

Toyosaburo Taniguchi
Former chairman and president
Toyobo Textile Company

Tatsuzo Mizukami
President
Japan Foreign Trade Council, Inc.

Tadahiro Iwakoshi
President
Nissan Motor Company

THE JAPAN-U.S. ASSEMBLY

VOLUME II

Proceedings of a Conference on
the Threat to the World Economic Order

American Enterprise Institute for Public Policy Research
Washington, D. C.

THE JAPAN–U.S. ASSEMBLY is the annual meeting of the Conference Board on U.S.–Japan Economic Policy. The assembly is operated by its executive committee in cooperation with the American Enterprise Institute for Public Policy Research. The chairman of the executive committee is Professor Paul McCracken.

EXECUTIVE COMMITTEE

Paul W. McCracken, chairman, Edmund Ezra Day university professor of business administration, University of Michigan

Milton Friedman, Paul S. Russell distinguished service professor of economics, University of Chicago

Hendrik S. Houthakker, professor of economics, Harvard University

Chiaki Nishiyama, professor and director, Center for Modern Economics, Rikkyo University

Miyohei Shinohara, professor of economics, Seikei University

Tadao Uchida, professor of economics, University of Tokyo

STAFF

Fusako Etoh, senior coordinator

ISBN 0-8447-2082-8 (Paper)
ISBN 0-8447-2083-6 (Cloth)

Library of Congress Catalog Card No. 75-883

© 1976 by American Enterprise Institute for Public Policy Research
1150 17th Street, N.W., Washington, D. C. 20036

Printed in the United States of America

MAJOR CONTRIBUTORS

Morris A. Adelman
Professor of Economics, Massachusetts Institute of Technology

Masao Baba
Professor, Institute of Economic Research, Kyoto University

Robert E. Baldwin
Professor of Economics, University of Wisconsin–Madison

C. Fred Bergsten
Senior Fellow, International Economics, Brookings Institution

Richard N. Cooper
Professor of International Economics, Yale University

James S. Duesenberry
Professor of Money and Banking, Harvard University

William Fellner
Sterling Professor of Economics, Emeritus, Yale University
Resident Scholar, American Enterprise Institute

J. Marcus Fleming
Deputy Director, Division of Research and Statistics
International Monetary Fund

Gottfried Haberler
Galen Stone Professor of International Trade, Emeritus, Harvard University
Resident Scholar, American Enterprise Institute

Irving B. Kravis
Professor of Economics, University of Pennsylvania

Edward J. Mitchell
Director, National Energy Project, American Enterprise Institute

Chiaki Nishiyama
Professor and Director, Center for Modern Economics, Rikkyo University

Takuji Shimano
Professor of Economics, Gakushuin University

Egon Sohmen
Professor of Economics, University of Heidelberg

Herbert Stein
A. Willis Robertson Professor of Economics, University of Virginia

Robert Triffin
Frederick William Beinecke Professor of Economics, Yale University

Tadao Uchida
Professor of Economics, University of Tokyo
Chairman, Econometrics Section, Japan Economic Research Center

CONTENTS

FOREWORD

The Japan–U.S. Assembly was organized in 1973 and held its first symposium in Tokyo in April 1974. It has been made possible primarily through the generosity of Mr. Toyosaburo Taniguchi, the former president of the Toyobo Textile Company in Osaka. Mr. Taniguchi has long held the belief that the way the world economy works is going to depend heavily on the nature of the economic relationships between Japan and the United States.

The activities of the Japan–U.S. Assembly have been aided by such leading businessmen as Mr. Tatsuzo Mizukami, the former chairman and president of the Mitsui Trading Company, Mr. Yoshizane Iwasa, the former chairman and president of the Fuji Bank, Mr. Koji Asai, the former president of the Sumitomo Bank, Mr. Tadahiro Iwakoshi, the president of the Nissan Motor Company, and others who share Mr. Taniguchi's belief.

The importance of the economic relationships between Japan and the United States is, of course, statistically obvious. These are now the two great economies in the free world. Together they account for upwards of 40 percent of the total gross national product in the free world. They also account for a very high percentage of free world trade.

It is our belief that the importance of these relationships is not merely statistical. The purpose of the Japan–U.S. Assembly is to deepen mutual economic understanding between the two countries in order to promote better coordination of their economic policies. The assembly's symposia are to be held annually for ten years, with participants who are primarily economists from the United States and Japan. It is highly desirable to have something like an annual meeting for discussions of pertinent economic questions from the Japanese and the American viewpoint and, through Mr. Taniguchi's generosity, these annual meetings are now under way.

It should be made clear, as my colleague Professor Nishiyama has pointed out, that our purpose is not to present American views of Japan or Japanese views of the United States, but Japanese economists discussing Japanese problems (or discussing world problems from a Japanese perspective) and U.S. economists discussing U.S. problems (or discussing world problems from the U.S. point of view).

The assembly is operated by its executive committee in cooperation with the American Enterprise Institute for Public Policy Research. The institute was our host for this 1975 meeting in Washington. We wish to thank them for their hospitality, and we wish to thank all who participated in the program, and especially our colleagues who came from Japan.

PAUL McCRACKEN
Chairman
Executive Committee
Japan–U.S. Assembly

INTRODUCTION

As president of the American Enterprise Institute, it was my pleasure and privilege to open the second meeting of the Japan–U.S. Assembly. We at AEI were delighted to have the opportunity to be hosts to this important effort to ensure continuing dialogue between two great countries.

The scholars who participated in this symposium were in part sharing the fruits of their ongoing research, in part debating the interpretations their colleagues have placed upon the data, in part reflecting on the world economic order from points of view tempered by long experience both in the academic world and in the world of policy making. They did not, of course, agree on all points, and even when there was substantial agreement, there were differences on details. Nevertheless, with a few exceptions, there seemed to be a clear consensus on the threat to the world economic order and on the underlying strengths of the system.

I had the good fortune to attend the first session of the Japan–U.S. Assembly in Tokyo in 1974. The proceedings of that conference were published by the American Enterprise Institute in 1975, under the title, *The Japan–U.S. Assembly: Proceedings of a Conference on Japan–U.S. Economic Policy,* with introductions by Paul McCracken and Miyohei Shinohara. In my view, it is particularly appropriate that Professor McCracken should have provided the introduction to that volume and the foreword to this one. Any significant idea comes to fruition through the efforts of dedicated people, and the Japan–U.S. Assembly is the brainchild of two such people, Professor McCracken from the United States and Professor Nishiyama from Japan. At AEI we are proud that Professor McCracken is chairman of our Advisory Board and coordinator of our academic affairs.

We had hoped to have the ambassador from Japan with us for the opening session of the assembly, but he was then recovering from surgery and we were fortunate to have as his representative the Honorable Seiya Nishida, minister extraordinary and plenipotentiary. I would like to echo Minister Nishida's hope that these meetings of the Japan–U.S. Assembly can light a torch to examine the economic future of a world where the economic present is sadly in need of light.

WILLIAM J. BAROODY
President
American Enterprise
Institute

OPENING REMARKS

It is a great honor and privilege for me to make these brief remarks at the opening of this session of the Japan–U.S. Assembly.

Last week we witnessed the Washington Cherry Blossom Festival, although the weather in Washington, which I experienced for the first time, was windy and cold. Yet this Cherry Blossom Festival symbolizes the warmth and friendship of the long-existing U.S.–Japan association. Now, in the wake of that festive occasion, we get together for serious academic and practical discussion on economic analysis and policies, with the participation of economic scholars representing both Japan and the United States.

At the moment, the proper assessment of the economic situation and the proper diagnosis for its treatment is a difficult problem for both government and economists. I am fairly new to the Washington scene, but ever since I came to this country, I have witnessed the difficulties the United States government has faced with the economic problems of inflation, recession and unemployment.

When I arrived in the United States last summer the unemployment rate was approximately 5 percent, whereas in about five or six months' time it reached 8.7 percent. Right after President Ford took office in August 1974 the main purpose of his economic policy was to contain inflation, and he made inflation "public enemy number one," but in a few months' time he had to change his emphasis to unemployment—it was a "179 degree change"—to focus on the depression and unemployment question.

The phenomenon with which he had to deal is not limited to the United States. Japan and Western Europe also face recession and unemployment under sluggish economic conditions. There are strong outcries from our business community in Japan that we should loosen the present tight money policy aimed at inflation control. Unfortunately, it is difficult even for leading economists to work out a common economic policy and it is difficult for them to visualize the future economic outlook from existing conditions. Many economic estimates, government as well as private, have had to be revised in recent times.

There are many outstanding Japanese scholars attending this meeting, and many outstanding scholars from the U.S. academic community, as well as from the administration. They are here to discuss problems of mutual concern for Japan and the United States, and through these discussions to focus on the difficult situations that must be faced worldwide. Of course, the Organization for Economic Cooperation and Development (OECD) and other international organizations are taking up these problems, but I welcome and congratulate the American Enterprise Institute and the Conference Board on U.S.–Japan Economic Policy for organizing such a forum at this time.

We in the Japanese government who are carefully following world economic trends are looking for some sort of recommendation or guideline so that we can learn from the present discussion and have a torchlight to brighten our future in the present dark world.

April 7, 1975

SEIYA NISHIDA
*Minister Extraordinary
and Plenipotentiary*
Government of Japan

PART ONE

THE THREAT TO THE WORLD ECONOMY FROM INFLATION AND RECESSION

THE THREAT FROM
INFLATION AND RECESSION:
THE CASE OF JAPAN

Tadao Uchida

The severe inflation and recession now prevailing in the world economy have produced several problems that had not been experienced since the end of World War II. This paper describes and analyzes some aspects of the present stagflation of the Japanese economy as that stagflation relates to the world economic situation.

First, the paper evaluates the recent inflation and recession in terms of the Japanese econometric model, concluding that it is impossible to explain the present economic dislocation without considering the drastic disturbances and structural changes for the economic system as a whole. Second, the paper examines the present upsurge of the threat from recession and inflation as it relates to production trend, price development, and international trade. We find that, while the stagflation phenomenon has many common facets throughout the advanced countries, there are some differences in individual nations. Third, the paper forecasts the future course of the stagflation for the Japanese economy, and from an international context suggests new threats in prospect.

Econometric Evidence of Recession and Inflation in Japan

In fiscal 1973 (April 1973 to March 1974) the Japanese economy expanded satisfactorily in the first half of the year, but with the "oil shock" the rate of production increase declined in the latter half, and the annual rate of economic growth was limited to 6 percent. Sharply rising prices were already in evidence before the oil shock, and they were additionally spurred by the energy crisis. The rate of increase for the wholesale price index and consumer price index in fiscal 1973 amounted to 23 percent and 16 percent.

Fiscal 1974 was a year of typical stagflation for Japan, with severe recession and inflation. As is clearly shown in Tables 2 and 3, the decline in production was so severe that the annual growth rate for fiscal 1974 was about −1 percent at best. The estimated rates of increase for the wholesale price and consumer price indices were 24 percent and 22 percent respectively.

Incidentally, the Tanaka cabinet had implemented the Socio-Economic Fundamental Plan in which the Japanese economic pattern during the five years

3

from 1973 to 1977 was determined through the medium-term econometric model. It was estimated that during the planning period the annual rate of economic growth might be 9.4 percent, and the rate of increase of wholesale and consumer price indices might be 2.3 percent and 4.9 percent. This being the case, there have been great discrepancies between the planned values and actual ones.

From the viewpoint of econometric analysis, the discrepancies between planned and actual figures may consist of three components: first, a revision of statistical information which was used to estimate the model; second, errors in the assumed values for exogenous (data and policy) variables; and third, discrepancies from the model building itself, such as structural changes and disturbances in the equation system. If we assume that the first factor is not serious, the remaining two factors should explain the differences at issue. Table 1 presents the details.

As for the second factor, it may be noted that while the plan assumed an expansion rate of world real trade at 8 percent per annum during the planning period, in fact world real trade, after having increased at a rate of about 13 percent in fiscal 1973, expanded at about a 5 percent rate in fiscal 1974. On the other hand, world manufacturing export prices, assumed to rise at a 2.6 percent annual rate during the planning period, suddenly accelerated, with the result that their rate of increase reached 21 percent in fiscal 1973 and 28 percent in fiscal 1974. These overseas developments in themselves would have stimulated the expansion of Japanese exports. Their favorable effects, however, have to some extent been cancelled out by the lessening of the export drive in the domestic industry and the secular strengthening of the yen against foreign currencies.

In the plan, import price movements were scheduled to be limited to a 3.2 percent annual rate. Influenced by the world inflation and especially by the oil crisis, the rate of increase of import prices had accelerated to 34 percent in fiscal 1973 and 50 percent in fiscal 1974. This naturally put upward pressure on domestic prices and cooled down total effective demand.

These two changes were important but they were not the only changes. Domestic economic patterns have also been subject to alterations. Above all, the government adopted restrictive demand policies in both the monetary and the fiscal area. In the plan, government capital formation was expected to increase at a 15.5 percent annual rate (in real terms) in order to improve deferred public welfare. The actual performance was quite different, however, and the reduction of the rate of increase of government real investment to −7.6 percent annually in fiscal 1973 and −2.5 percent annually in fiscal 1974 helped press down total demand significantly. In the meantime, monetary policy also turned in a tightening direction, resulting in a rise of the official interest rate to 9 percent—which was never dreamed of in the plan.

How these factors, together with others, changed real GNP from what was planned may be seen through the use of the econometric model: the results are

4

Table 1

ACCURACY OF JAPAN ECONOMIC RESEARCH CENTER (JERC) MODEL

(in percent)

	GNP		Wholesale Prices		Consumer Prices		Wage Rates	
	1973	1974	1973	1974	1973	1974	1973	1974
------- Differences between Actual and Planned Figures -------								
Overall percentage change	−4[a]	−11[a]	+39[b]	+56[b]	+10[b]	+27[b]	+13[b]	+32[b]
Portions of Differences between Planned and Recalculated GNP, Explicable by Structural and Nonstructural Factors								
Source of differences								
Export circumstances	+237	+135	—	—	—	—	—	—
Import prices	−91	−60	—	—	—	—	—	—
Effective demand policies	−213	−197	—	—	—	—	—	—
Other data changes, etc.	+218	+159	—	—	—	—	—	—
Sum of nonstructural factors	+151	+37	+12	+22	+14	+15	+9	+15
Structural changes	−251	−137	+88	+78	+86	+85	+91	+85
Sum of explained differences[c]	−100	−100	+100	+100	+100	+100	+100	+100

a Represents difference between actual and planned rate of growth.

b Represents difference measured against planned values.

c Sign (+ or −) indicates direction of difference.

Source: Japan Economic Research Center (JERC) Econometric Model.

5

entered in Table 1. If we assume no structural changes and disturbances since the plan's implementation, the recalculated figure for GNP should coincide with the actual figure. However, as is clearly indicated in Table 1, the recalculated GNP in both 1973 and 1974 exceeded the planned value to a considerable degree. This means that we must take into consideration the existence of severe structural changes as well as disturbances contributing to the suppression of the level of activity in the Japanese economy in two consecutive years.

The same procedure was applied to the movement of prices and the wage rate. Here also we found that the recalculated figures were quite different from the actual, though here the recalculated figures were smaller. When econometric analysis was applied to each price equation, it was found that the planned and calculated figures moved closer. Thus, 28 percent of the gap between the planned and actual was explained by inserting the realized values of explanatory variables into the wholesale price equation in fiscal 1973, and 45 percent was explained by the same procedure for fiscal 1974. However, a large unexplained part still remained. The situation was quite different for the case of consumer prices. Almost 100 percent of the gap was accounted for when the actual values of the explanatory variables were taken into account. These results indicate that, while the behavior of wholesale prices may have changed to a great extent, the behavior of consumer prices has remained stable.

This procedure, which we will call a "partial test," can be also applied to other structural equations to find which behavior has remained stable and which has not. Generally speaking, the economic behavior of business enterprises— inventory accumulation, fixed capital formation and wage determination—seems to have withstood structural change fairly well. It should be added that a downward shift in the propensity to consume might have occurred in 1974. Certainly it would be difficult to explain recent economic dislocation without considering some factors which have come into existence in recent years. And since the situation in Japan seems to be more or less similar to the situation in other advanced countries, the December 1974 statement of the OECD (Organization for Economic Cooperation and Development) about the widespread lack of business confidence may be suggestive.

The OECD *Economic Outlook* pointed out a number of economic problems, the following seeming to be the most important: (1) the uncertain outlook for economic activity, (2) the lack of confidence in the ability of governments to control the serious and manifold impact of the energy crisis, (3) doubt whether the market economy and financial institutions can continue to function properly at a continuing high rate of inflation, (4) the behavior of consumers, in turn related to uncertainties resulting from both inflation and unemployment, and (5) uncertainties regarding structural adaptations implied by the energy crisis.

The Present Threat: International Comparisons

The present stagflation assailing the Japanese economy seems to be a phenomenon common to all advanced countries, though its strength may differ somewhat from country to country. Decline in production, increase in unemployment, and a rise in prices are the main characteristics of stagflation. This is clearly shown in Tables 2 and 3 for Japan, the United States, West Germany, and the United Kingdom.

The stagflation may be the result both of structural dislocation and of restrictive demand policies in the domestic area, but there is no doubt that the oil crisis should be counted as one of its important causes. The oil crisis, starting with the embargo on the export of petroleum, turned later into the formation of an international cartel on oil prices. A sudden soaring of energy prices occurred in the international market, adding a new problem in the world economy—a problem of large deficits in the trade balance of non-oil-producing countries and a problem of recycling huge amounts of petro-dollars accumulated in oil-producing countries.

Statistics in Tables 2 and 3 outline the story for four countries. Each country is troubled with an increase of unemployment accompanied by a decline of production activity. In the United States and West Germany, inflation is much milder than in the two other countries, though unemployment rates are approaching the intolerable point. In Japan and the United Kingdom, while the unemployment is not so serious, inflation is unbearable.

As for the position of the international balance of payments, every advanced country except West Germany is afflicted with an excess of import increases over export increases, mainly from the sudden deterioration in the terms of trade. However, the deficit in the current balance will fortunately be smaller than anticipated. For example, the $40 billion deficit expected in all OECD countries in 1975 may be reduced to a $30 billion deficit. Moreover, it is shown in Table 4 that the tendency for import increases to exceed export increases has grown weaker as time goes on.

Careful examination of Tables 2 through 4 indicates the subtle differences in stagflation for each country. The trade-offs differ from one country to another: in some, price movements vary with the pressure of demand, while in others, changes in unemployment are not so sensitive to the decline of production. Countries also have different external balances in accordance with their international competitiveness. Moreover, public opinion in each country may attach different weights to the goals of economic policy as the economic situation changes. Thus, the United States is now greatly concerned with unemployment, whereas the United Kingdom has to seek measures to mitigate both the high rate of inflation and the deterioration in the international balance of payments. West Germany, after succeeding in stabilizing the price level, is going to turn to an expansionary policy

Table 2

INDUSTRIAL PRODUCTION CHANGES AND LEVELS OF UNEMPLOYMENT, FOUR MAJOR INDUSTRIAL COUNTRIES, 1973–1975

	Year-end '73	Year-end '74	Jul. '74	Aug. '74	Sep. '74	Oct. '74	Nov. '74	Dec. '74	Jan. '75	Feb. '75
Industrial Production (percent change from 12 months earlier)										
Japan	+17.5	−2.4	−1.4	−6.1	−6.7	−9.9	−12.4	−15.1	−18.0	—
United States	+9.0	−0.9	−0.9	−1.0	−0.9	−1.7	−4.5	−6.5	−9.3	−11.6
West Germany	+7.4	—	+1.3	−2.8	−5.5	−4.1	−3.6	−9.9	—	—
United Kingdom	+7.1	−3.0	−1.3	−1.0	−2.4	−3.2	−2.7	−2.2	—	—
Levels of Unemployment (in percent)										
Japan	1.3	—	1.2	1.1	1.4	1.3	1.4	1.6	2.0	—
United States	4.9	5.6	5.3	5.4	5.8	6.0	6.5	7.2	8.2	8.2
West Germany	1.3	—	2.2	2.3	2.4	3.0	3.5	4.2	5.1	—
United Kingdom	2.6	—	2.6	2.7	2.7	2.7	2.7	2.7	3.0	—

Source: Organization for Economic Cooperation and Development, *Main Economic Indicators*, various issues.

Table 3

PRICE CHANGES, FOUR MAJOR INDUSTRIAL COUNTRIES, 1973–1975
(percent change from 12 months earlier)

	Year-end '73	Year-end '74	Jul. '74	Aug. '74	Sep. '74	Oct. '74	Nov. '74	Dec. '74	Jan. '75	Feb. '75
					----Wholesale Prices----					
Japan	+15.8	+31.4	+34.2	+32.8	+30.6	+28.7	+25.1	+17.0	+10.4	+5.6
United States	+13.1	+18.9	+20.4	+17.8	+19.7	+23.1	+23.5	+20.9	+17.2	+14.6
West Germany	+6.7	+13.4	+13.9	+14.1	+14.2	+14.6	+13.4	+12.4	+10.3	—
United Kingdom	+7.3	+23.4	+25.1	+25.8	+26.1	+27.0	+27.7	+28.0	+31.7	—
					----Consumer Prices----					
Japan	+11.8	+24.4	+25.2	+25.4	+23.8	+26.2	+25.8	+21.9	+17.0	+13.7
United States	+6.2	+11.0	+11.5	+11.0	+12.0	+12.0	+12.1	+12.2	+11.7	—
West Germany	+6.9	+7.2	+6.9	+7.0	+7.3	+7.1	+6.5	+5.9	+6.1	—
United Kingdom	+9.1	+16.0	+17.1	+16.8	+17.1	+17.1	+18.3	+19.2	+19.9	—

Source: Organization for Economic Cooperation and Development, *Main Economic Indicators*, various issues.

9

Table 4

CHANGES IN EXPORTS AND IMPORTS, FOUR MAJOR INDUSTRIAL COUNTRIES, 1973–1975

(percent change from 12 months earlier)

	Year-end '73	Year-end '74	Jul. '74	Aug. '74	Sep. '74	Oct. '74	Nov. '74	Dec. '74	Jan. '75	Feb. '75
Exports										
Japan ($)	+29.4	+50.3	+56.5	+70.8	+42.0	+63.5	+43.5	+41.3	+41.5	+30.6
United States ($)	+43.9	+38.5	+41.6	+38.5	+29.1	+31.6	+31.7	+25.6	+32.3	—
West Germany (DM)	+19.8	+29.2	+40.6	+29.9	+26.2	+19.4	+18.4	+33.9	—	—
United Kingdom (£)	+27.8	+32.4	+38.1	+38.8	+35.0	+33.9	+21.7	+29.0	+50.0	—
Imports										
Japan ($)	+70.9	+62.3	+71.3	+50.7	+46.1	+43.2	+38.6	+29.5	+26.0	−6.8
United States ($)	+24.4	+46.2	+55.0	+58.1	+50.9	+44.0	+37.3	+48.4	+48.8	—
West Germany (DM)	+13.0	+23.2	+32.6	+39.4	+32.5	+20.4	+17.5	+23.6	—	—
United Kingdom (£)	+42.4	+45.9	+59.1	+38.6	+37.7	+28.0	+33.2	+25.8	+31.3	—

Source: Organization for Economic Cooperation and Development, *Main Economic Indicators*, various issues.

to stimulate domestic production. In what follows, we will concentrate attention on recent economic movements in Japan and consider the present state of the threat from stagflation and the countermeasures that may be adopted against it.

Compared to the decline in other countries, the fall in industrial production in Japan is conspicuously high. The percentage decrease in the production index reached −15.1 percent (annual rate) in December 1974 and −18.0 percent (annual rate) in January 1975. In spite of the large decline in production, the unemployment rate remained at a low level, less than 2 percent. This may be an incredible figure from the viewpoint of the United States, and some explanation of this unique characteristic of the Japanese economy may be necessary.

Following are some reasons why there is such a low level of unemployment with a drastic decrease in production. First, there is room for reduction in the number of hours worked. Traditionally, working hours in Japan have been long enough to allow slashing of hours in a depression period. For example, regular hours worked in December 1974 declined by 5 percent (year-to-year change) and overtime worked declined by as much as 26 percent. Second, there are many daily workers, temporary workers and part-timers, and housewives who are not counted as unemployed when they are dismissed. In Japan, moreover, there still are numbers of old-line workers who are self-employed or family-employed. These workers can find jobs in industry when industry is booming, but once the recession starts, they return to their native places where their traditional jobs are available. Third, there is the practice of the so-called "Japanese layoff." Lifetime employment is so popular in Japan that a firm will not discharge a worker even if he is given a layoff notice. In the layoff period, a worker is not engaged in a job, but he is employed by the company. Fourth, there is a downward flexibility in the wage rate. Because a bonus system is observed by Japanese companies, the total salary for the year is changeable through the adjustment of temporary payments. This helps to lower unit labor cost when a recession comes. Fifth and finally, there is selective monetary policy for firms losing money. When a company, be it small or large, gets into difficulty, financial institutions make an effort to protect it from bankruptcy.

All this being the case, the low rate of unemployment is compatible with the fall in industrial production, and unemployment does not become a serious social problem in Japan. This, in turn, enables the government to adopt drastic restrictive demand policies in order to stabilize the rate of inflation.

As production adjustment goes on, a change in the rate of inflation appears, and wholesale prices decline in absolute terms. This happened at the end of calendar 1974 and has continued up to the present (April 1975). In February 1975 the change in wholesale prices over the previous year was 5.6 percent. The present downward movement of wholesale prices is almost the same as in the past, and this reflects the competitive character of the market mechanism in Japan. The same thing may be said, though less strongly and with some time-lags, about consumer price behavior. It is needless to say, however, that with heavily declining production, company profits have eroded considerably. The average profit/sales ratio in all industries fell by 30 percent in the latter half of fiscal 1973 and is at 1.5 percent for fiscal 1974, compared with its usual level around 3 percent.

Another change brought about by the decline of production may be found in the position of the international balance of payments. We have already noticed that the tendency for imports to exceed exports has been modified gradually in recent months. Tables 4 and 6 show the figures. The current balance for fiscal 1973 was $3.9 billion in the red, and the basic balance of the same year showed a $13 billion deficit. Some improvement in both balances seems quite sure for fiscal 1974 (April 1974 to March 1975). For example, the current balance deficit will contract to the $1.7 billion level, and the basic balance will show only a $4.3 billion deficit.

The improvement in the international balance of payments may be the result of two main factors. One is the export drive and reduction of imports caused by the decrease in domestic production, the other the weakening of the yen against foreign currencies. Besides these, we can add the introduction of the government's restrictive policy against international capital movements, which stimulated the inflow of capital and restricted outflow.

Thus, the three parts of the threat to the Japanese economic order—unemployment, inflation, and imbalance of payments—seem to be capable of being met, though perhaps not entirely satisfactorily. In the background there lies the following policy mix. For the unemployment problem, the flexibility of the Japanese employment structure makes it possible to overcome social unrest. The problem of inflation can be coped with by the usual restrictive demand policies with the aid of the competitive market mechanism. The international balance-of-payments problem can be met partly by the flexible exchange rate system and partly by direct control of capital movements. In summary, the complexity of the Japanese tradition and the room for adjustment mainly resulting from the past high rate of economic growth can contribute to mitigating the threat from recession and inflation.

Other advanced countries should be able to find their own way out from stagflation. According to the degree of their success in conquering their difficulties, it may be that 1975 will be different from the past two years. What are the prospects for 1975?

New Problems in Prospect

Prospects for the world economy are still uncertain, but not so bleak as they looked a while ago. In the near future, new problems will come on the field, and each country will have to tackle them. Let us take up the matters in Japan first, and then follow the new difficulties in their international context.

As a clue, let us take the short-term economic forecast for Japan. Table 5 includes the forecast for the Japanese economy for fiscal 1975 by the Japan Economic Research Center (JERC), of which I am a chairman in the econometric section. According to this forecast, the Japanese economy should recover in 1975, but at a real growth rate of only 2.6 percent. The forecast assumes adoption of a stimulative monetary policy and positive public work programs in the first half of the year. However, under the assumption that a structural change has occurred and the investment function and consumption function have shifted downwards, the response of the private sector is uncertain. We cannot expect quick recovery in the near future. This is quite a different situation from the past when rapid recovery was the ordinary course of things after the turning point.

If this forecast is correct, certain troublesome problems appear in the domestic economy. With stagnant production for a while, there will be an easing of the demand-supply relations in the labor market, and this will change potential into actual unemployment. It already has been pointed out that Japanese "cushion" has worked in the labor market so as to absorb the redundant labor force. If much more pressure is applied to the present labor market, this cushion may stop functioning and there will be an actualization of unemployment all at once. Unlike the United States or some European countries, Japan has not done much toward preparing countermeasures and institutional settings against actualized unemployment. In this case, there may be social and political unrest in Japan beyond comparison with that in other countries.

The other problem which may arise from a slow recovery is a problem of international trade. In accordance with the slow pace of production recovery, the movement of Japanese imports will be stagnant. The volume of imports for fiscal 1975 is forecast to decrease at the rate of 2.6 percent. Because of the heavy dependency of exports from Southeast Asian and Pacific Island countries upon Japanese imports, the decline in Japanese imports will reduce the exports of those countries and this, in turn, will aggravate the recession in the overseas area near Japan. (If we measure the export dependency by the percentage ratio of the export to Japan from each country over the country's total export, the figures for 1973 were as follows: Republic of Korea 39 percent, Formosa (Taiwan) 19 percent, Hong Kong 10 percent, Malaysia 18 percent, Philippines 36 percent, Indonesia 54 percent, Thailand 26 percent, Australia 32 percent, and New Zealand 10 percent.) In this way, the slow tempo of Japanese economic expansion will generate international difficulty. Its symptoms have already appeared in the statistics for January 1975, where several countries' exports to Japan have fallen considerably from those last year.

Now let us turn to Table 6 and consider the Japanese external balance-of-payments position for fiscal 1975. With a low rate of economic growth, a large surplus may be seen on the trade and current balances ($11.5 and $5.6 billion

Table 5

JAPAN'S 1973 (ACTUAL), 1974 (ESTIMATED), AND 1975 (FORECAST) GNP, INDUSTRIAL PRODUCTION, AND PRICES, WITH YEAR-TO-YEAR RATES OF CHANGE NOMINAL (N) AND REAL (R)

(GNP components in trillion yen)

	Fiscal Year 1973			Fiscal Year 1974			Fiscal Year 1975		
	Value	N	R	Value	N	R	Value	N	R
Personal consumption expenditures	Y 59.2Tril	+20.6%	+5.7%	Y 72.5Tril	+22.4%	+2.5%	Y 84.3Tril	+16.4%	+4.8%
Government current purchases	10.4	+23.7%	+6.3%	14.1	+35.0%	+3.5%	17.0	+20.7%	+4.0%
Private housing investment	9.8	+39.8%	+12.1%	10.2	+3.7%	−9.4%	12.2	+19.7%	+10.3%
Private plant & equipment investment	22.3	+33.4%	+13.9%	23.2	+3.9%	−13.3%	23.7	+2.4%	−4.5%
Private inventory investment	4.0	+98.4%	+71.7%	3.7	−6.9%	−31.0%	1.1	−69.4%	−70.8%
Government capital formation	10.5	+10.7%	−7.6%	12.3	+17.4%	−2.5%	14.1	+14.7%	+5.5%
Exports	13.2	+22.9%	+6.1%	20.8	+57.7%	+24.5%	22.8	+9.8%	+5.7%
Imports (subtract)	14.2	+61.8%	+24.8%	21.4	+50.5%	+4.9%	20.8	−2.6%	−2.6%
GNP	Y115.2Tril	+21.7%	+6.1%	Y135.4Tril	+17.5%	−0.8%	Y154.6Tril	+14.2%	+2.6%
Industrial production index (1970 = 100)	131.6		+14.8% R	120.2		−8.7% R	112.2		−6.7% R
Wholesale price index (1970 = 100)	125.4	+22.6% N		154.9	+23.5% N		164.9	+6.5% N	
Consumer price index (1970 = 100)	131.0	+16.1% N		159.6	+21.8% N		178.1	+11.6% N	

Source: Japan Economic Research Center (JERC).

Table 6

JAPAN'S 1973 (ACTUAL), 1974 (ESTIMATED), AND 1975 (FORECAST) BALANCE OF PAYMENTS

(in billions of $U.S. with year-to-year percentage changes)

	Fiscal Year 1973	Fiscal Year 1974	Fiscal Year 1975
Trade balance	+0.8	+4.4	+11.5
Exports	+39.0 (+32.3%)	+58.2 (+49.5%)	+66.0 (+13.4%)
Imports	−38.2 (+80.8%)	−53.8 (+41.1%)	−54.5 (+1.3%)
Current balance	−3.9	−1.7	+5.6
Basic balance	−13.0	−4.3	+2.6

Source: Japan Economic Research Center (JERC).

15

forecast, respectively). This will cause trouble. In the first place, since the surplus will contribute to making the yen stronger, there will be a decreased volume of export and at the same time an increased volume of import, so that the domestic recovery may be delayed to some extent. Of course, the surplus in the international balance of payments works to increase the domestic monetary supply unless the central bank takes neutralization measures. The surplus will not be so large in the basic balance, however, because of the net outflow of capital from Japan.

In the international picture, the surplus in the current balance in Japan means a deficit of the same amount in overseas countries. Even if this year's current-balance deficit for all OECD countries will be much smaller than anticipated, the Japanese surplus may be high enough to produce troubles in international cooperation. Moreover, the bilateral imbalance between countries will invite political difficulties of the sort experienced between the United States and Japan in the early 1970s. In any case, further increases in international friction may not be able to be evaded.

The best way for Japan to proceed will be to take positive measures for expansion and to raise the real growth rate as high as possible. But it is easier to preach than to practice. First of all, the present Miki cabinet, unlike the Tanaka cabinet, is reluctant to engage in expansionary policy. Secondly, even if stimulative measures are employed, there is some doubt that private enterprises will react positively, since business confidence has been lost for a long time and firms are not seriously promoting capital formation. The same may be true for consumer behavior accompanied by the uncertain prospects for both inflation and unemployment. Notice the low forecasts for the rate of increase in consumption and investment expenditures in Table 5.

Thirdly, there is a strong reason for the government to be hesitant about expansionary policy, and that is the possible revival of inflation. Though the rate of inflation is slowing down, there still are many potential forces that will push up the general price level in the future. For two successive years, firms have suffered losses from rising units cost and declining profit margins. They are eager to raise prices, if demand expansion comes. At the same time, there is a danger of bottleneck inflation accompanying recovery since the growth of potential capacity has been insufficient as a result of stagnant investment activity.

This being the case, the lull the Japanese economy now is undergoing may be ended by domestic and international factors. Moreover, the world economy may have in common with Japan the things that have been mentioned here. The slow recovery from recession is a phenomenon not only for Japan but for other advanced countries. The prolonged state of unemployment may be a headache for the United States in the coming two years. It is past experience that, if world production does not increase, the world trade will be retarded accordingly. The graph

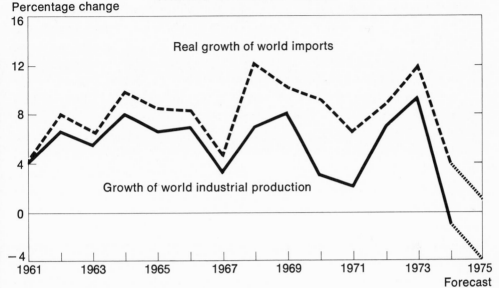

Figure 1

TRENDS IN WORLD TRADE

Percentage change

Real growth of world imports

Growth of world industrial production

1961　1963　1965　1967　1969　1971　1973　1975
Forecast

Source: Japan Economic Research Center (JERC).

presented here shows the possibility of a large decrease in world trade in 1975. If this happens, the prospects for world economic recovery will be lessened.

In the international balance of payments, the contrast between surplus countries and deficit countries will become greater. While the surplus of the oil-exporting countries will not grow, some of the non-oil-producing countries, like West Germany and Japan, will keep or enlarge a surplus, and some other countries continue a deficit, so that an adjustment of the international balance of payments may be complicated indeed. In present circumstances (in which the functions of the International Monetary Fund [IMF] and General Agreement on Tariffs and Trade [GATT] have been chipped away) it is not an easy matter to deal with this new disequilibrium. It must be added that the threat of protectionism may also appear even in a traditionally free-trade country like the United Kingdom to cope with the dilemmas of unemployment and deficit.

Finally, even if the world economy regains prosperity in due course, the fear of inflation will come up again. What is the future of energy and food prices? What is the likelihood of demand-pull and cost-push inflation? What are the prospects for the international movement of inflation? All is vague in a mist, and we cannot eliminate the potential threat from inflation, even though price movements subside temporarily.

With these prospects, this year of 1975 may be more difficult to handle than last year was. Restrictive demand policy has been a powerful measure against

17

inflation and the energy crisis, and its ill-effect on employment has been dealt with so far. However, it will not be so easy in the future as it has been in the past. We have arrived at the point of "no retreat" and must depend on expansionary policy. But we do not know definitely what the implications of this policy are.

THE THREAT FROM INFLATION AND RECESSION: AN OVERVIEW

Richard N. Cooper

I will begin with some general observations on the world economy, follow with some comments on the American economy, and then return to the world economy and prospects for trade.

Professor Uchida's paper contains a sentence that is especially appropriate for opening my remarks. He says that "all is vague in a mist." We live today in a world of extraordinary uncertainty—not just the uncertainty that ordinarily attends economic transactions among countries and within countries in a world in which we cannot forecast perfectly, but uncertainty that derives from the fact that the conventions and even the formal rules which have provided the framework in which these transactions take place either have broken down or are under severe pressure. They no longer provide a stable framework in which commercial transactions can take place.

This condition reflects what I would call "system uncertainty," involving much wider bounds for uncertainty than would normally be the case. Excluding the world war, one would have to go back to the early 1930s to find a comparable period of system uncertainty. Let me here mention three areas in which this system uncertainty exists, and then three causes for the uncertainty. The three areas are international monetary conventions, the law of the sea, and inflation. The three causes of the uncertainty are technological change, anti-colonialism, and problems of government policy.

The most obvious area of uncertainty is the Bretton Woods Agreement, which laid down the formal rules governing financial relations among countries. It is now virtually in abeyance. We now have floating exchange rates rather than fixed exchange rates. We do not have official convertibility of any currency into gold or into other currencies at a fixed price, although happily we retain convertibility in the market sense of the term. Happily also the procedural features of the Bretton Woods Agreement have not yet broken down. We still have arrangements for discussing disputes among nations.

The movement to reform the monetary system got off on a nonproductive track, and we are now living in a period of interim arrangements. It is not clear where we are going to go from here, and indeed, though it is sometimes said that we have moved to a system of flexible exchange rates, that is not an accurate description even of the present arrangements. We have floating exchange rates, but we do not have a system of floating exchange rates: we do not have any system at all. We have practices, even de facto arrangements, but no system. The absence of a system means that those engaged in international transactions do not know with reasonable probability what the system will be like two or five years from now, and as a result they cannot plan ahead within a known framework. We have a formal charter in the area of trade, the General Agreement on Tariffs and Trade (GATT), which goes back to the 1940s but that, too, has been badly eroded.

The process has been a prolonged one, and unfortunately it is not merely the rules of behavior that have been eroded. The procedures themselves are not working the way they were intended to work or the way in which they have actually worked in the past. Many countries feel freer than they once did to manipulate their trade policies without holding themselves accountable to the international community.

A second area, which is not normally associated with the world economy but which is symptomatic of the erosion of conventions, concerns the law of the sea. Conventions that have governed use of the seas for over two centuries are now threatened. There is a strong tendency today for territorial extension into what was once regarded as the high seas, giving rise to great uncertainty about the rights and responsibilities of those concerned with oil exploration, mineral exploration, fishing, and even navigation. The world's largest official conference has met in Geneva to discuss the law of the sea, but there seems to be very little tendency toward a convergence of views.

Finally, inflation itself gives rise to an enormous amount of uncertainty, partly because inflation on the scale on which we now observe it is a new phenomenon. The uncertainty arises in part because we do not know whether unemployment is going to continue at present rates or fall or increase, but also because many of our national conventions and laws—the tax systems for most countries (Canada now excepted), interest rate laws, and commercial contracts—are written in nominal terms. These laws and conventions provide the framework for commercial undertakings. At rates of inflation such as we have observed in the past several years, these conventions and laws are not tenable in the long run, but we do not know yet when or exactly how they will be changed.

That also adds to uncertainty, so I think that Professor Uchida's phrase is a particularly apt one: "All is vague in a mist." We do not know what the framework will look like several years from now.

Three reasons for this uncertainty should be mentioned. First, there have been technological developments. I use "technology" in a broad sense here, in which the emergence of the Euro-market is a technological development. Many technological developments and many market developments were not anticipated when the rules and conventions were laid down. In the financial arena the most important development concerns the international mobility of capital. In the law of the sea, it has to do with our capacity to exploit the ocean so that what once was regarded as an inexhaustible resource is now quite exhaustible, and free access to the sea is no longer a tenable arrangement.

Second, many countries of the world regard these conventions and formal rules as suspect for having been laid down, as historically they were, in a colonial era. They assume these rules and conventions to be infused with a subtle colonialism. The less developed countries have now almost made it a point of pride to question everything that has been inherited from the past, on the grounds that, since it was inherited from the past, it must be against their interests.

One can see this clearly in the Law of the Sea Conference. One can see it in a much more muted form in the discussions of international monetary reform and of trade arrangements. The breakdown of procedural arrangements in the GATT was largely brought about by the refusal of less developed countries to adhere to them. There is a kind of new spirit of solidarity among these countries and an eagerness to question all existing conventions.

Finally, it is unclear how, and how rapidly, governments will react both to the choice between inflation and recession and to the need to come to terms with the inflation that will be with us for some period of time. The governments are themselves uncertain not only about the nature of their reaction but even about its direction. This creates a continuing source of uncertainty for the private economy. As Professor Uchida pointed out, our forecasting techniques for consumer and investment behavior are especially difficult to apply at the present time.

After these general observations let me turn to the more immediate question of world recession and inflation. The current recession is the first clear example—one can have some debate about what happened in 1958—of a policy-induced recession. The recession which we are now in was desired by governments. They did not forecast it accurately, they did not appreciate how deep it would be, but the contractionary tendencies that led initially to the recession were deliberate actions of policy in order to damp down world inflation. The recession has of course been greatly aggravated, to a degree that is still underestimated by many GNP forecasters, by the increase in oil prices.

It is a technical fact that most of our forecasting models are not set up to handle changes in the terms of trade. With the increase in oil prices, we have encountered a severe worsening of the terms of trade for most oil-consuming nations—all those that have not been fortunate enough to produce some other commodity such as sugar whose price has risen as much as the price of oil. The change in the terms of trade creates a discrepancy—which again has not been adequately noticed—between real incomes and real expenditure.

The point has been correctly made that as long as the OPEC countries are not spending their new income, the oil-consuming countries need not make the real transfer resulting from the increase in oil prices. We can continue to spend at the old level, borrowing from the OPEC countries in order to support the expenditure. But while this is perfectly true, it is also true that real incomes have fallen even while real expenditure need not fall. The distinction between income and expenditure is important because it is not merely private firms and individuals but also governments that draw a distinction between spending out of income and spending borrowed funds.

It is necessary in the short run to spend borrowed funds, but one of the risks to the world economy is the anxiety that the spending of borrowed funds generates and the policy actions that it may induce, a point to which I will return later. Before doing that, I want to make another distinction, one concerning inflation. It is the distinction between a change in the price level, in particular an increase in the price level, and a change in the rate at which prices increase. Our statistical measurements during the period of change of price level do not reveal any such distinction. Prices are going up, and if one defines inflation simply as any observed rise in prices, of course the two are both "inflation." But from a policy point of view there is a very great difference between a once-for-all change in the price level and an acceleration of the rate at which prices increase year after year.

What we observed in 1974 was a combination of the two, with the combination varying from country to country. Let me focus for the moment on the change in price level. We had a large increase in oil prices and in food prices; for both reasons—once-for-all change and acceleration—price levels were raised markedly, visibly, and disconcertingly. But because both these reasons obtained we should expect a decline in the rate of price increase in 1975, 1976, and subsequent years. We should not expect a further fourfold increase in oil prices nor, with any luck at all, a further doubling of food prices such as we experienced between the fourth quarter of 1972 and the fourth quarter of 1974. It is therefore not surprising to see a sharp drop in the rate of price increase such as that we are now observing. It has very little to do with the world recession. It results from the fact that in 1973–1974 we had some important price increases that were once-for-all. This being so, the rate of price increase must necessarily drop substantially in 1975. It is no cause for surprise and no cause for congratulation.

The linkage between the two varieties of price increase comes in the response of factor incomes to changes in the prices of goods, and there the experience has varied markedly from country to country. A number of countries have formally indexed factor incomes. In these cases, what starts out as a once-for-all change in the price level is built into factor prices, and that, of course, feeds back into costs and commodity prices. An endless wage-price spiral can start from what was initially a once-for-all change.

One can see this especially in Europe. Wage settlements in Italy and the United Kingdom are in the high teens or the low twenties. Wage settlements in a number of smaller European countries have been above 15 percent. The one country that has notably succeeded in preventing high commodity price increases from being translated into factor income increases has been West Germany, where—thanks to the "social bargain" of Chancellor Helmut Schmidt—key wage settlements in 1975 have been extraordinarily moderate, given what has happened to prices in general. It must also be said that West Germany kept its price increases down partly through revaluation of the Deutschemark.

The United States is not far off. Wage settlements were amazingly moderate through the spring of 1974, given what happened to prices—and in fact in the United States, alone among major countries, real wages fell. Since last summer wage settlements have accelerated. Average settlements rose from 6 to 7 percent a year to 10 to 11 percent a year, in spite of the fact that unemployment has been high and rising during that period. This phenomenon is quite out of the realm of our past experience and suggests that the cost of living catch-up element is a much more powerful influence on wage settlements than unemployment rates are, at least in the short run.

In any case, countries have varied a great deal in their success in keeping the once-for-all increase in prices from being translated into higher factor incomes. For some countries, what started out as a once-for-all inflationary impetus has become, I fear, a continuing impetus to wage increases.

There is in addition one further consequence of this distinction between once-for-all increases and acceleration that is worth mentioning, and that consequence concerns the money supply. A once-for-all increase in the price level that is not accommodated by an increase in the money supply gives rise to a reduction in the real value of the money supply. During 1974 all the leading countries of the world, with the interesting exception of West Germany, experienced a substantial reduction in the real value of the money supply. This phenomenon offers a further cause for the depth of the recession we are now in. The real value of financial assets has fallen substantially because of this once-for-all increase in prices.

Now, in my view, whatever the source of inflation, once it is built into factor price increases, it is in practice exceedingly difficult to work out of the system. One could, of course, run a depression that was severe enough to bring factor price increases to a halt, another Great Depression. But a depression of the required depth is politically intolerable in all democratic countries. This being so, once factor prices begin to increase we have to reconcile ourselves to the fact that some inflation will be with us for a long period of time.

The demand-induced inflation in the United States in the late 1960s stepped up factor price increases by three to four percentage points right through the recession of 1970–1971. I fear that the round of inflation we had in 1973–1974 will lead to another step-up in the rate of factor price increases to the 8 to 9 percent range, in spite of the current recession. It will take a long time to work that out of the system. Many other countries find themselves in a much worse position in that regard, with wage increases at 15 percent or above.

For that reason—and I say this with resignation rather than with any satisfaction—I think that we must gear our economic laws, regulations, and conventions to what has become a regrettable but nonetheless certain fact of the late 1970s and early 1980s: we will have rates of inflation much higher than existed in the period from 1969 to 1972. U.S. inflation during the rest of the decade will not be at the high rates of 1973–1974, with their once-for-all components, but will be higher than in previous years. So we must make some accommodation to that. Furthermore, this prediction suggests that flexible exchange rates will be with us for a long time to come, simply because experience has varied so much from country to country.

Let me turn now from these observations to the topic in the title, "The Threat from Inflation and Recession." First, what does it mean to say that the world economy is threatened? Surely there will be a decline in world trade in 1975 in real terms, because of the recession. The growth in the value of trade in the last two years has been extraordinary. Most of the growth, however, was in prices. No doubt the growth in value will continue this year but on a declining volume because of the recession.

The real threat to the world economy comes through national policies. Given the "system uncertainty" that I discussed earlier, there is a tendency for nations to go it alone, to withdraw from what is increasingly perceived as an untrustworthy world economic system. As a point of departure, it is worth recalling some of the events in the late 1920s and early 1930s and what happened as the world economy slid into the Great Depression. There are a number of similarities today, though also important differences.

There was a recognition, then as now, at least by some countries, that there was a world economy—that an increase in tariffs, in particular, would not generalize and would be self-defeating if all countries increased tariffs. In 1927 an abortive attempt was made to call a tariff truce among countries when it was perceived that several countries were moving towards restrictive tariffs. The problem began in agriculture, where demand slackened before it did for industrial goods. The attempted truce did not work. In February 1929, before the great crash, India imposed tariffs on textiles; in March 1929 France and Italy imposed tariffs on automobiles. Then in early 1930 Australia adopted an across-the-board increase in tariffs.

That was the first major tariff move. In the United States what was the most tremendous tariff increase in our history was working its way through Congress. The Hawley-Smoot tariff became law in June 1930, and when that was passed, all hell broke loose. Many countries protested the passage of that tariff and urged

President Hoover to veto it. He did not veto it, and within the next four months about twenty countries adopted higher tariffs, sometimes selective, sometimes general, in response to the Hawley-Smoot tariff. Switzerland even attempted an embargo of American goods.

In early 1930, before the Hawley-Smoot tariff was passed, twenty-seven countries attended the conference in a second attempt to call a tariff truce. The United States was not among them. Eleven countries of the twenty-seven signed the agreement, but only seven ratified it, reflecting the rapid erosion of the situation.

The tariff then was seen primarily as an instrument of domestic policy, an instrument to be used to increase employment. One of the happy differences between then and now is that we now know of much more powerful instruments for generating employment, in particular the manipulation of monetary and fiscal policy, so that today we do not have the same compelling domestic reasons for increasing tariffs. Nonetheless, I think that we cannot entirely rule out tariff increases. In 1969–1971 in the United States organized labor made a very strong claim for protective tariffs. That pressure was resisted and we now have the Trade Act of 1974, which, I hope, will put that kind of protectionism to rest for awhile.

There is still the problem of agriculture. The problem of agriculture started the difficulty in the 1920s and we have the problem of agriculture today. Last year, when grain prices were rising and beef prices were falling, Canada, the European Economic Community, and Japan all imposed restrictions on imported beef, and Australian beef came flooding into the United States because Australia's other markets were closed. There were very strong pressures here to impose restrictions on beef imports into this country. These pressures were transmitted to Australia.

That represents the beginning of an unraveling which one can see even these days. More serious concern, however, stems not from particular industry problems (they will always be present in recessions), but from the anxiety I mentioned earlier about spending borrowed funds instead of spending out of one's own income. Just as tariffs are not so attractive as an instrument of domestic policy as they were in the 1920s, they are also not so attractive as a measure to improve the balance of payments now that we have flexible exchange rates. Nonetheless, countries are anxious about their enormously large trade deficits—not payments deficits, but trade deficits—and about the need to borrow in order to sustain them.

In the aggregate the need to borrow abroad is a very clear and unambiguous one. As long as the OPEC countries are not spending the full amount of their oil revenues on imports, the rest of the world must borrow in order to sustain its trade deficits, its extra payments for oil. At the same time there is anxiety over borrowing to sustain those trade deficits, an anxiety reinforced by an international community that still has not gotten over the idea that balance-of-payments deficits or balance-of-trade deficits are bad things, that countries that run them are to be chided for their misbehavior, and that pressure should be put on these countries to bring their position into better shape.

In particular, I have in mind Italy, which has recently been identified as the "weak sister" among the major industrial countries. Italian economic policies during the last several years are subject to criticism, but it is also true that if one were to put Italy's trade balance on a full employment basis and allow for the oil price increase, there would be little wrong with Italy's trade balance. Italy's trade deficit is largely explicable by the increase in oil prices, the recession in Germany (Italy's major market) that began in 1973, and the subsequent recession in the United States and in France.

So the most serious threat to the world economy at the present time is made up of anxieties about borrowing to sustain trade current deficits and an international ethic that does indeed frown on trade deficits. In 1974, Italy did impose a 50 percent advance deposit requirement on imports. Happily that was removed a few weeks ago. A few weeks ago, however, Finland imposed a 15 percent import surcharge. These are danger signs.

Both the International Monetary Fund (IMF) and the Organization for Economic Cooperation and Development (OECD) are conscious of the problem of generalization—the "adding-up" or "consistency" problem—and are constantly reminding countries that they have to pay attention not just to their own position but also to the position of countries generally. That is a useful reminder. I hope it works. Nonetheless, it is important for all the leading countries to recognize that they have to borrow these days to sustain current account deficits, that there is nothing wrong with current account deficits, and indeed that for the oil-consuming nations they are absolutely necessary. The suggestion has even been made to set formal targets for these deficits and to allocate targeted deficits on a country-by-country basis. It is perhaps not necessary to go that far, but the underlying point is an important one.

Inflation also carries its dangers for trade and its threats to the world economy. In the Great Depression, restrictions on exports were imposed mainly by less developed countries trying to raise foreign prices for their products. Recently we have seen restrictions put on exports in order to reduce domestic prices. The United States, for example, restricted exports of hides in 1966, and (more important) exports of soybeans, fertilizer, and scrap metal were all restricted in 1974 in order to keep domestic prices down. But of course that restriction raised prices abroad. As with import restrictions to reduce trade deficits, these actions, if they are pursued by many countries, are self-defeating from the viewpoint of the global economy. We need restrictions on restrictions of this kind.

In summary, the dangers to the present world economy stem first from the existence of a high degree of "system uncertainty" which tends to induce nations to retreat from reliance on the system and to rely more on their own actions; and, second, from the temptation under present circumstances to try to improve trade balances, one way or another, in a period in which improving trade balances is collectively impossible as long as OPEC is not spending all of its money, and, similarly, in more isolated instances, from the temptation to impose export restrictions for domestic economic reasons. In other words, we run a risk of withdrawal into neo-isolationism and a growing unwillingness to be concerned with international cooperation—and concern with international cooperation is for many countries a good functional substitute for truly system-oriented behavior.

The key steps to avoid these dangers are, first, for the United States to retain its system-oriented behavior, a retention we have shown some tendency to retreat from since 1971, and second, for Japan and Germany as the second and third largest trading economies to move away more rapidly than they have done from what I would call the "small country psychology," the assumption that if demand weakens at home it can always be made up through export expansion.

That is true for a small country; it is no longer true for Japan. The figures that Professor Uchida gives for Japan's current trade surplus are really frightening, as he suggests, from the point of view of the world economy. Germany is in a similar position. It is not possible for the second and third leading countries to run large trade surpluses these days without putting enormous strain on the system as a whole, given the high oil prices and the need for industrial countries generally to run trade deficits.

Third, but not least, a key step is to get the world economy out of its present recession as rapidly as possible and back onto a reasonable economic path, necessarily at a higher rate of inflation, not than in 1973–1974, but than we had during 1969 to 1972; and for that reason also necessarily with floating exchange rates.

COMMENTARY

Irving B. Kravis

I think it might be useful to look at the historical record. This is my way of taking refuge from the difficulties I find myself in.

The first speaker presented an econometric analysis which I am unable to duplicate, and the second speaker thought in very large terms, so my refuge is to think small. I would like to call your attention to what has happened to world trade and production in the last fifty or seventy years, and to try to find what the association has been between world trade and world inflation or world depression.

Let me start by saying the statistical data we have on this subject are terrible. We really do not know what has happened to prices in the world economy. We have figures on the value of world trade which diminish in reliability as one goes back in time. And even for the recent period, we really do not know what the movement of prices in world trade has been. What are usually called price indices for world trade are not price indices at all but unit value series, and for manufactured goods, which now account for nearly two-thirds of world trade, the validity of unit values as a measure of prices is extremely dubious.

Now, like other economists, having carefully described how worthless the statistics are, I will go ahead and use them. I will, however, make one concession to the poor quality of the data by using price measures for world trade that are really price measures—but not, I regret to say, measures of prices in world trade. I am referring to the U.S. wholesale price index. It seems to me that for one who is desperate for a price series giving some clue to what might have happened to prices in world trade, resorting to the movement of U.S. wholesale prices is preferable to using unit values.

Still I must confess I do not escape from unit values completely, because I am going to cite statistics on the physical volume of world trade which were obtained by deflating total values of world trade (dollar values) by unit values. In any case, for what it is worth, the story runs something like this. Adapting Professor Cooper's terminology—I am not sure I agree with it entirely—you might say that if you look at the past hundred years there have been two jumps in wholesale prices in the United States and one sharp but more gradual upswing.

The two jumps correspond to the two wars and (barring what happened within the war periods) these price jumps had very little impact on the volume of world trade. That is, the postwar volume in each case was not markedly different from the prewar volume. The sharp but more gradual upswing in prices began in the mid-1960s, and by 1974 there had been a 70 percent increase in wholesale prices since 1964.

This compares to a rise of about 40 percent in the first jump (World War I), and nearly 100 percent in the second jump (World War II). This recent 70 percent upswing has been associated with a large expansion in the real volume of world trade. The physical volume, as near as we can measure it, has doubled. This rate of increase was about the same as the rate of increase in the preceding decade. Thus we have had twenty or twenty-five years of unprecedented expansion in the volume of world trade, and this expansion appeared to be unaffected by the movement of prices. That is, the sharp increase in inflation following 1964 did not appear to make very much difference in the rate of expansion of world trade.

Looking on the other side of possible price movements, at recession rather than at inflation, we have (fortunately) only one experience to point to—the Great Depression of the 1930s. Our measure suggests that the physical volume of world trade declined about a fourth from the 1929 peak to the depth in 1932 or 1933. In this period it is clear that the impact of the depression differed on different components of trade.

The quantity of agricultural products in world trade did not diminish very sharply, but prices collapsed. In the manufacturing sector, the adverse effect on prices and quantities was more evenly distributed between the two. Thus, as Professor Uchida suggested in his paper, the main relationship one finds for world trade and the world economy as a whole is that there is a close association between world trade and world production, though that association has not been uniform in the past.

Apparently, in the period before World War II, the rate of expansion of world trade tended to be somewhat slower than the rate of expansion of world production. Since World War II, the physical volume of world trade has probably increased at a faster rate than the physical volume of world production. One can speculate on the reasons for this: certainly it is obvious that, with the modern technology for transportation and communication, the world has grown smaller, and this might explain the change in the ratio of world trade to world production.

Now I would like to turn to policy questions. It seems to me that one can point more clearly to the impact of the past on public policy in the case of the Great Depression than to the impact of inflationary periods on public policy for world trade.

The depression had a scarring effect on the attitudes of developing countries toward world trade, particularly in Latin America. This was the continent where more than anywhere else producers of raw materials and primary products were independent countries, though some would say that their independence was only nominal. But they had at least some degree of jurisdiction over their own monetary, fiscal, and commercial policies, and what these countries saw was that the sources of their export proceeds, which they relied upon to finance imports of raw materials, capital goods and in some cases even food, disappeared from under them. The impact of this lesson can be given in five words: do not rely on trade.

This view was soon bolstered by the theories of Prebisch, Singer, and Myrdal, theories that portrayed not only the cyclical instability of trade, but, more particularly, a set of secular trends and structural conditions that made it unwise for developing countries to place much reliance on trade. The result was the dominance of import substitution policies in the development strategies of most LDCs—policies which have only recently begun to lose their charm. Thus the impact of the Great Depression on the policies of developing countries lasted for three decades after the depression was over.

Looking toward the future, I would like to take a slightly more optimistic view of the situation than was taken by my colleague, Professor Cooper. This has two dangers. First of all, I am afraid that whenever Professor Cooper and I disagree, he is likely to be right. Secondly, when it comes to a choice between optimism and pessimism it is always wiser for an economist to select pessimism. Nevertheless I will persist in my disagreement with him.

On the question of system uncertainty, I would like to argue that the degree of system uncertainty that we have today may be larger than in the past, but that if one turns the question around and asks during what periods did we have system certainty, we find that it is not clear the world was a certain place at many points in the history of the past half-century. One important source of increased uncertainty that Professor Cooper did not mention, though it was implicit in one of the things he said, is the diminution in the power of the United States.

That diminution creates all kinds of uncertainties. It is partly responsible for and partly attributable to the ganging up of the developing countries, in which they are using their organized political and economic power in efforts to obtain a better economic deal from the West. But I think one can argue that the very shrinkage of the world has created a greater realization that countries are in the same boat and has lessened the likelihood that countries will adopt policies that are damaging to their neighbors. This is especially true of the big countries, including, obviously, Japan and West Germany. The other large developed countries are showing more and more signs of the same kind of responsibility for the welfare of the world economy that the United States began to evince in the 1940s and England many decades earlier.

There are specific examples of the growth of responsible community behavior. The behavior of central bankers during the past fifteen or twenty years, for example, shows remarkable flexibility. They have not, it is true, been very good at designing a long-run system that will settle present and future problems, but it has been no small achievement for them to have avoided disaster in coping with the crises that have emerged in a rapidly changing world economy. Their great achievement has been to keep the monetary aspect of the international economic system from interfering with the real aspect. There is ground for considerable satisfaction and perhaps even optimism in contrasting the mind set and behavior of the central bankers of today with those of the central bankers in, say, the 1920s.

Even on the trade side I am not sure that I see deterioration. The present looks threatening if we forget how bad the past was—if, for example, we think of the past in terms of the great American visions of a free-trading world. We fought hard to get the Havana Charter adopted, but after it was adopted we did not ratify it. When GATT became operative (supposedly on an interim basis) one of the first things that happened was that the United States placed itself in violation of GATT by maintaining quotas on dairy imports.

This was in the first few years after the war. We had this great design for free trade, one that we really rammed down the British and other throats, and then the first thing we did was turn around and say, "We have to get a waiver, because we are in violation of GATT." Other countries were quick to follow our example. No country throughout the history of GATT ever refrained from doing what it wanted to do for domestic reasons, no matter what the GATT arrangements were.

I do not think the present period shows countries regarding their trade obligations under GATT any more lightly than they did before. All along the game under GATT has been not to do anything that is going to hurt anybody else, unless you want to do it very much. If you want to do it very much, then you go ahead and do it and accept the consequences. The main consequence is that your representative in GATT will be called upon to do some explaining: he may be embarrassed, but your domestic interests will still have their cake. The value of GATT has been simply that it has enabled countries to avoid doing things that are not important to them but are important to someone else. That was true in the 1950s and it has not changed.

Indeed, even on the trade side there have been some innovative and beneficial things that have happened. I hesitate to use this example in an audience that is a meeting of Americans and Japanese, because I think "voluntary" export restraints must be one of the bad words in the economic lexicon of Japanese discussions of international trade—justifiably so because the Japanese were badly burned on the first example of these voluntary export restraints, the cotton textile agreement.

Although I have no desire to defend these voluntary export restraints, they represent a considerable advance over the unilateral quotas or other kinds of restrictions that might otherwise have been used. At least they involve consultation that really is consultation. Consultation under the GATT ordinarily consists of calling the fellow on the other side and saying, "We are going to raise the tariff on your goods or withdraw this concession tomorrow." A voluntary export restraint at least really does require consultation and negotiation. Furthermore, the sting is taken out of it by the fact that the monopoly profit on the licensed export goes to the businessmen of the exporting country, rather than to recipients of quotas in the importing countries.

I believe that one of the most important new problems that face us today is the political power of the developing countries, and particularly the heady example that has been given to the developing countries by the success of the oil cartel. There is not only a desire to imitate in the form of whatever additional cartels can be devised, but also a clear example of the success of government intervention in markets. It appears that a new feature of the world economy will be an increased role of governments in the organization of commodity markets. What happens to prices and quantities not only in oil but also in iron and steel, bauxite, phosphates, and so on, seems likely to be determined to a much greater degree than in the past by intergovernmental negotiation.

I do not expect any good to come of this. I think that in general the origin of exports will be determined by the political power of countries and their negotiating strengths rather than by economic considerations. On the other hand, I do not expect any great breakdown in the world economy. I would like to suggest that Professor Cooper's advice to Japan and West Germany not to regard themselves as small countries might in this regard be extended to the United States. That is, I think the United States, ridden with guilt over being rich and having in the past been so powerful, has tended to lie down and say, "You can walk over me for a while." I do not believe the United States should use its power in an exploitative way, but neither do I believe that the United States should be quite as complacent as we have been in the face of some of the more outrageous claims that the developing countries have made.

It has never been demonstrated that the structure of the world economy or of world trade operates against the interests of developing countries as has been alleged. By and large, unwise internal policies of the LDCs have prevented them from sharing fully in the growth of world trade in the past twenty-five years. Among the LDCs, the countries that have had good per capita growth rates have tended to have open economies, and the evidence is that the line of causation runs from internal growth to trade rather than from good or bad luck in export markets for traditional goods to fast or slow growth. The LDCs have the normal inclination to blame their difficulties on outsiders, but economic growth is mainly a function of internal factors.

I think that we have to recognize that there are great problems between the developing countries on the one hand and the developed countries on the other. But I believe one can see in the events of the past ten or fifteen years evidence of responsibility toward the world economy on the part of the developed countries that gives slightly more cause for optimism than Professor Cooper has expressed.

Before closing I would like to push this question of system uncertainty a little further in the monetary area. There is no doubt that there is a lot more uncertainty about what the monetary system is going to be like a few years down the pike than there was in the middle 1950s. I can believe that this creates uncertainty for the International Monetary Fund in deciding what its rules should look like on the record. And it is also inconvenient for me because I have to change my lecture notes more often than I otherwise would. But the real question is the practical consequences of this, either in the world of policy makers or in the world of trade and capital movements.

I think that, in the second area, one sees a great difference between the impact of the Great Depression on trade quantities and the impact of the termination of dollar convertibility in August 1971 or of the big change in prices in 1973 and 1974. The Great Depression played havoc with world trade; the uncertainties of flexible exchange rates and the international monetary system have not thus far had any visible impact on trade.

Before it is worthwhile for us to say that past or prospective changes in the position of the dollar or changes in the monetary system really create uncertainty that matters, we have to point to specific areas where this uncertainty has practical consequences.

Robert E. Baldwin

The combination of recession and inflation affects world trade and economic activity generally in two ways. First, the level of trade and production is reduced, and, second, the relationships among components of these economic activities are altered. Recession by itself produces both of these effects, but distortions in the composition of trade and output are magnified by the existence of inflation together with recession.

Dr. Uchida, in his excellent paper, illustrates these points by referring to the estimations of GNP and other variables based on the econometric model of the Japan Economic Research Center. As he notes, a part of the wide gap between estimated and actual values in 1974 can be accounted for by incorrect assumed values for the exogenous variables reflecting the general level of economic activity and government policy. However, a significant difference between predicted and actual values is still left after the introduction of new and more appropriate values for the exogenous variables. This, as he notes, is the result of structural changes in the set of equations underlying the model.

In part, the structural changes are undoubtedly shifts in such factors as prices and income levels, but, as Dr. Uchida points out, there apparently have been important changes in the economic behavior of consumers and businessmen. For example, investment and consumption functions may have shifted downward. It is changes of this nature that give the forecaster and policy planner the most difficulty. Businessmen and consumers simply do not now behave in the same way they used to behave towards a given set of variables. A period such as the recent past—when confidence has been badly shaken—will alter behavior.

Though we relearn this lesson during each period of serious disruption, we seem to forget it shortly and begin predicting the effects of various policy actions as if people would behave as in the past. Dr. Uchida rightly emphasizes this point in cautioning about the results of expansionary policies in Japan. It is equally applicable to other countries and should make us hesitant in predicting just what will be accomplished here by the recent tax cut.

Another aspect of the structural changes associated with stagflation lies in the differential impact of stagflation on the trade patterns of the various countries. For example, Dr. Uchida estimates that, because of the low growth rate in 1975, Japan's trade surplus will rise from $4.4 billion to $11.5 billion. The trade position of the United States might likewise be worse but for the recession. The volume of oil imports in particular is at a comparatively low level both because of the slack in domestic activity and because of price factors. The fact that U.S. wholesale prices have risen less than those in countries such as the United Kingdom and Japan has contributed to the good U.S. export performance in recent months. When the recession ends, we must be prepared for a reversal in some of these favorable factors and consequent significant relative changes in exports and imports as well as in exchange rates.

Not only does the combination of recession and inflation in itself greatly reduce and distort world trade, but another threat lies in the adoption of certain policies in response to these twin evils—policies which have the effect of further reducing and distorting trade. One point that Dr. Uchida mentions, and on which I would like to elaborate, is the tendency of governments to pursue protectionist policies in the face of the current economic difficulties.

Fortunately, the existence of flexible exchange rates has not only been an enormous aid in adjusting to changed economic circumstances but also an aid in helping to relieve the pressures for protectionism. Nevertheless, protectionist pressures are still strong. The AFL-CIO in this country, for example, is beginning to make a vigorous effort to prevent any significant tariff cuts under the current round of GATT-sponsored multilateral negotiations. Unions in other industrial countries—the United Kingdom in particular—are apparently mounting similar campaigns.

In past negotiation it has only been possible to make crude estimates of the effect of various tariff-cutting rules on U.S. employment, both in aggregate terms and on a detailed industry level. The data collection problem was viewed as simply too costly for the relevant government agencies to undertake. However, three developments have occurred to make this view no longer accurate.

Most important has been the collection for eighteen major industrial countries of detailed trade and tariff data over recent years (on a comparable basis) by the GATT secretariat. The second has been the publication of an input-output table for the United States on a 367-sector basis. Previously the government only published a 79-sector table. Finally, there have been considerable efforts in recent years to estimate import-export demand elasticity on a fairly detailed industry basis.

Using these three sets of data, together with the labor coefficients relating output and employment on a detailed industry basis, I recently completed some preliminary estimates of the employment effects in the United States of a significant tariff cut by the industrial nations.

Excluding commodities currently subject to quantitative controls—that is, textiles and oil—it turns out that a 50 percent linear cut—that is the same cut made in the Kennedy round, if made by all these eighteen industrial nations, the major trading countries in the world—actually would tend to increase total employment in the United States slightly.

With a fixed exchange rate—of course, it is not fixed, but one can make the assumption and then change the exchange rates to get the total effects—the 50 percent tariff cut increases employment in this country by something like 14,000 jobs and has a $37 million surplus effect on the balance of trade. Both are really negligible figures, even without taking into account the fact that the cuts could be made over ten years. You can say that the effects on employment and the balance of trade are negligible: there is no great improvement and certainly no great worsening. When the impact of the cuts in reducing the trade diversion caused by the EFTA and EEC trade agreements is also taken into account—the first estimates do not take it into account—the picture becomes somewhat more favorable to U.S. labor but not significantly so.

Of course, there are certain industries that will be adversely affected by the tariff reductions. My calculations indicate that in 40 of the 310 industries in which trade takes place employment will decline by at least one-half of 1 percent of the industry's labor force. However, if we phase the cuts over ten years, normal industry growth and quitting rates will make it possible for us to absorb the cuts without any involuntary unemployment in all but sixteen of the forty industries. Moreover, this probable unemployment is not only small absolutely—on the order of something like 20,000 jobs in the sixteen industries—but speaking comparatively, it is less than the 30,000 jobs created in industries where employment rises by one-half of 1 percent or more as a result of the 50 percent cut.

Of course, I have not taken into account the consumer surplus benefits, but even if one takes a strongly pro-labor position—namely, that one does not want to cause any involuntary unemployment—it seems that the industries that will be hurt are nevertheless very few in number. The ones we all know about as being import-sensitive do show up in my study as industries that can be hurt by significant tariff cuts—ceramics, steel, footwear, and so on. But even in almost all these industries one could phase the cuts gradually over time without causing any major problems.

Now, in view of these figures it is difficult to see why we should not undertake a significant tariff cut and reap the consumer benefits of a better distribution of world resources. It is understandable why labor and many businesses are reluctant to cut duties in the face of a serious recession, but it is probably not even technically possible to put the cuts into effect before 1977 at the earliest. It would also be quite feasible to delay them further, should economic recovery not be achieved by that time. There is no reason we cannot postpone all these cuts until an appropriate time when the world economy is in fairly decent shape.

It appears, however, that those few industries that may suffer in employment—such as footwear and the steel industry—have convinced other labor groups to present a united protectionist front. Without active counterpressure, organized labor has thus been able to use our current stagflation difficulties to achieve a slight gain for part of its membership at the cost of larger potential gains to other parts of its membership and to consumers in general.

PART TWO

THE THREAT TO THE ECONOMIC ORDER FROM THE EMERGENCE OF CARTELS AND MONOPOLY POWER

THE ECONOMIC BACKGROUND
TO THE REVISION OF
JAPAN'S ANTI-MONOPOLY LAW

Masao Baba

"The core of the economic problem facing us today is the concentration of power in a few hands." This was written exactly ten years ago in Estes Kefauver's book *In a Few Hands* (1965). Needless to say, it was written about America, but these words have an urgent sound to us Japanese today. In September last year, Japan's Fair Trade Commission (FTC) published the "Proposed Main Points of the Anti-Monopoly Act Revision" as set out in Appendix A. Since then, discussions centering on these proposals have become increasingly vigorous, and voices for or against them have been heard from government offices, the political parties, financial circles, consumer groups, economists and legal academicians. Why must the present Anti-Monopoly Law in Japan be revised and strengthened? The main purpose of this paper is to clarify some of the aspects of the economic background to this question.

First of all, I would like to look at Figure 1. The solid line in the figure represents the index of the accumulated production concentration ratio for the top 3 firms in 121 manufacturing industries, using 1965 as the base year. Its movement is based on a simple arithmetic average. The line of dashes increased the coverage by about 50 industries, using the same method but using 1970 as the base year. In addition, the dotted line shows the average concentration ratio index, using 170 industries (in 1972 the total production of these 170 industries amounted to 60 percent of the total production of all manufacturing industries) weighted by the production of each industry.

Even from a quick glance at this figure, it is clear that industrial concentration in Japan has shown a remarkable increase in recent years, and I think it is fair to "guesstimate" that it has reached approximately the same level as is now seen in the United States and Europe. It is, of course, extremely difficult to carry out international comparisons of industrial concentration and the results are problematical. However, if we include consideration of the peculiarly Japanese situation, which is almost nonexistent in other countries, in which the tendency to form enterprise groups and "keiretsu" (enterprise interlocks) is particularly strong, we must conclude that the real level of industrial concentration is rather higher in Japan than in the United States or Europe. It has already been established that the oligopolistic system in such industries as iron and steel, automobiles, electrical

Figure 1

CHANGES IN PRODUCTION CONCENTRATION RATIOS IN JAPANESE INDUSTRY

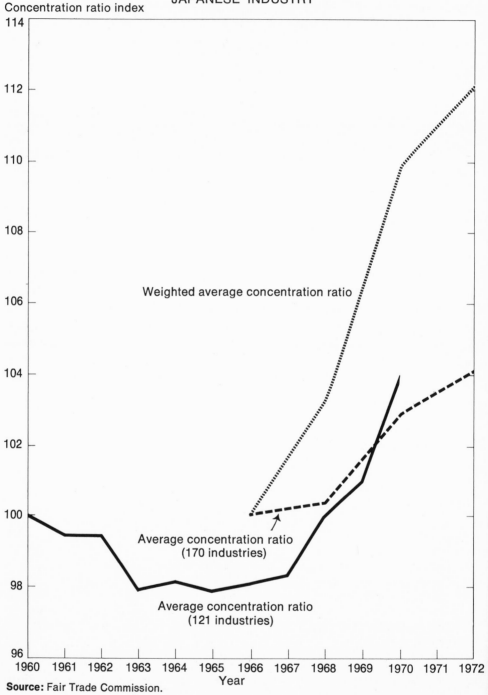

Concentration ratio index

Weighted average concentration ratio

Average concentration ratio
(170 industries)

Average concentration ratio
(121 industries)

Year

Source: Fair Trade Commission.

machinery, and chemicals has become highly stabilized, but recently the degree of monopolization has increased rapidly in the foodstuffs and paper and pulp sectors and the distribution and construction sectors.

Oligopoly can be divided into "collusive oligopoly" and "non-collusive oligopoly" depending on whether some form of collusive relationship exists among the companies. It is said that, until about 1965, many of Japan's oligopolistic industries were to a large extent "non-collusive." In fact, it is accepted by many economists that this kind of company behavior, through its outstanding ability to adapt to changes in the economic structure, was one of the most important factors underlying the high rate of economic growth. However, it appears that, from about the time when the high rate of increase of industrial concentration began to appear (as seen in Figure 1), cases have increased in which Japan's oligopolistic industries showed a clear change in character from non-collusive (or competitive) behavior to collusive (or noncompetitive) behavior. Also, the effects of oligopoly are growing in various other ways. For example, an analysis of the average rate of price decrease by production concentration groups in recessions, carried out by Professor Kobayashi of Hokkaido University, makes it clear that in times of recession the rate of decrease in prices is smaller in the high-concentration-group industries than in the low-concentration-group industries. This tendency is clearly observable in the recessions of 1964–1965 and 1970–1971. That is to say, while prices in the highly oligopolistic industry group, where the top-three-firm concentration ratio exceeded 80 percent, were remarkably rigid downward, in the non-oligopolistic industries, where the concentration ratio was below 30 percent, the rate of price decrease was particularly high (see Table 1). Similar facts have been

Table 1
CONCENTRATION RATIOS AND PRICE RIGIDITY IN RECESSION PERIODS IN JAPAN

Concentration Ratio Group	Price Changes in Percent		
	1961–1962	1964–1965	1970–1971
Top three firms			
over 90 percent	5.1	4.1	0.6
80–89 percent	5.3	4.3	2.6
70–79 percent	9.3	4.4	7.8
60–69 percent	12.0	4.6	6.0
50–59 percent	10.2	3.9	8.8
40–49 percent	10.4	7.0	7.7
30–39 percent	12.8	10.6	4.3
20–29 percent	9.0	11.5	11.5
under 20 percent	18.5	14.5	15.1

Source: See text.

pointed out in research carried out by Mr. Hosoi of the Fair Trade Commission and the Japan Economic Research Center.

However, we must take note of the fact that recent movements of oligopolistic administered prices have not merely been rigid downward, they have also been more flexible upward than changes in demand or costs. Especially in the course of the rapid inflation of the last two or three years, Japan has become infested with many illegal price cartels, and as a result prices have been jacked up more easily, and moreover on a larger scale than in earlier years.

In the four years between 1971 and 1974 (the period covered in 1974 is from April to September) 132 of the 156 warnings issued for violations of the Anti-Monopoly Law dealt with illegal price fixing. Moreover, the present provisions for the punishment of these illegal acts are extremely unsatisfactory, and because policies designed to construct effective measures for the abolition of these cartels are not sufficient, the degree of control has not increased. Of the 156 violations mentioned above, 69 were repeated offenses, and an amazing fact is that 16 large companies were instructed more than three times to abandon their illegal activities.

In our free competitive economic system, conspiratorial groups are clearly more dangerous than villains who make mischief on their own. Activities which restrict competition are spreading—moreover, considering that the same company may be repeatedly committing violations against the Anti-Monopoly Law, it is not sufficient merely to strengthen the present stipulations for penal action against offenders. It would appear that we must, as soon as possible, establish a system in which excessive profits gained from monopolizing or restriction of competition are confiscated in full and illegal cartel behavior does not pay.

However, when monopolization of industry develops at a rapid pace, what happens as a result of barriers to entry or conscious parallelism is a situation which scarcely differs from monopolistic market control. Especially in industries where dominant-firm price-leadership exists, prices are formed as if there were absolutely no competitive relationship (that is, there is a monopolistic price) and it makes no difference how many firms there are in the industry or what percentage of production they account for. The number of industries in which the top-three-firm concentration ratio is very high and in which recent evidence of this kind of market behavior has been found has increased to a large extent. As examples, we may give dairy products, glutamin soda, mayonnaise, beer, nylon, synthetic rubber, dentifrices, photographic products, synthetic household cleaning products, plate glass, heavy rails, sheet pile, bricks, aluminum ores, cans used for food canning, automobiles, pianos, national newspapers, and so on.

We cannot expect to have competitive company behavior unless there exists a competitive market structure. Consequently, in order to deal sufficiently with the various ills which may result from a high degree of monopoly, it is necessary not only to strengthen the various regulations for the control of behavior in the

Anti-Monopoly Law, but also to make legal preparations to take steps to abolish monopoly (that is, to divide companies or transfer parts of their business) and so improve the market structure itself. It is my opinion that the logically inevitable conclusion to the revision of the Anti-Monopoly Law is a law that abolishes monopoly and supports and encourages competition, nevertheless avoiding the nationalization of industries. When we consider the regulation of market structure in this way it is of course necessary to take deliberate care that the steps taken do not greatly harm economies of scale (and similar advantages) of large firms. However, judging from the results of the measurements I have attempted up to now, the smallest optimum size of firms, with the exception of a very few industries (for example iron and steel, automobiles), is not very large.

As I briefly mentioned above, industrial groupings or "keiretsu" take on important meaning when we consider problems of concentration of economic power or restriction of competition in Japan. In particular, we must take note that stockholding by companies has shown a remarkable increase in recent times. At the end of 1965 the portion of the stock of all quoted companies held by domestic corporations was approximately 47 percent, while at the end of 1973 this percentage had reached 63 percent and the portion of stock held by individuals was little more than 30 percent. Compared to the United States or West Germany, where the portion of stock held by individuals is 70 percent, it must be said that this is an extraordinary state of affairs, and its economic significance and influence are great.

If we study each individual case, we can find the reasons for the existence of these stockholdings, such as the reconstruction of firms in which the management failed, investment in venture business or the exploitation of new industrial fields. However, if we consider it in basic terms, the major reason for a corporation's acquiring stock is to secure some kind of business advantage. If that is so, then there is an excessive concentration of economic power when, among the corporations with more than 10 billion yen capital or more than 200 billion yen total assets, some thirty own stock which exceeds their capital in value. Ever since the Anti-Monopoly Law was first enacted in 1947, Clause 9 of the law has prohibited holding companies as a matter of principle. Despite this fact, we may marvel at the situation in which many companies exist whose stockholdings are greater in value, in some cases many times greater, than their capital. "As long as it is a sideline, it does not matter how much stock an enterprise owns": with this kind of interpretation, Clause 9 of the Anti-Monopoly Law is becoming nothing more than a scrap of paper.

There are two problems which are especially worthy of note here. The first is the massive stockholding by the general trading companies and the other is the mutual intercorporate stockholding by companies within the same company grouping. According to the *First Report on General Trading Companies* (FTC, 1974),

45

the six largest trading companies owned stock in 5,390 quoted and unquoted companies at the end of 1972, and the companies which were majority-owned by them numbered 506: the six largest trading companies were the largest stockholders in 1,057 companies. Also the ratio of mutual intercorporate stockholding among the most important companies of the six largest company groupings—the Mitsui group, the Mitsubishi group, the Sumitomo group, the Fuji group, the Dai-ichi Kangin group and the Sanwa group—rose from 11.2 percent at the end of 1966 to 16.9 percent at the end of 1972. Especially in the old "zaibatsu" groups, Mitsui, Mitsubishi, and Sumitomo, the ratio showed an outstanding increase from an average of 14.8 percent to 22.9 percent in this period. According to the research carried out by the *Oriental Economist,* the ratio of mutual intercorporate stockholdings by the major companies of each major group was highest in the case of the Sumitomo group at 25.4 percent, followed in order by Mitsubishi, Mitsui, Sanwa, Fuji, and Dai-ichi Kangin.

In cases where one company owns stock in another company, a controller/controllee relationship can occur to some degree, but sufficient opportunities exist for cooperative or binding relationships in cases of mutual intercorporate stockholding as well. At any rate we cannot avoid thinking that effective competition will be weakened or destroyed by such stockholding. It is reasonable to think that the degree of intercompany collusion is all the greater in cases where even a small percentage of stock is held mutually by companies within the same group (especially when it is done with production and sales advantages in view, or accompanied by the dispatch of officers) than in cases where the percentage of stock held by one company is relatively large.

General trading companies have played an important role in the development of the Japanese economy, because they have had access to an extremely efficient information-collection mechanism. They have played a large part in the development of overseas resources and the introduction of new technology, and have acted as coordinators for direct overseas investment, and hence are worthy of praise. However, if they are strengthening the move towards "keiretsu" or improving their own position in the various company groupings to which they belong, and also are taking dominant advantage of borrowing power from financial institutions or purchasing large amounts of stock to strengthen the company groupings—and if by these means the concentration of economic power by company groupings raises barriers to entry—then we must apply stringent controls over the ownership of stock by the major companies within these groupings and in particular by the general trading companies.

The role played by financial institutions in the concentration of economic power by company groupings is even larger than that played by the general trading companies. The large banks own larger quantities of stock than the general trading companies and it is necessary for us to strengthen controls on this kind of stockholding. Of course control by financial institutions of ordinary companies can be effectively carried out by financing stock ownership. Consequently, it goes without saying that it is also necessary to strengthen controls in this direction.

According to FTC investigations, aggregate concentration in Japanese industry, measured by the capital concentration ratio of the top 100 nonfinancial companies, shows a slight downward trend from about 1963 on. However, we must take note of the fact that the increase in the number of corporations in this period was astonishing, the number rising from 464,519 in 1963 to 825,605 in 1969, and also that the rate of increase of capital for all other firms was much greater than that for the top 100 firms. In addition, according to research carried out by Mr. Iwasaki of Kōnan University on the top 100 firms by sales in the mining and manufacturing industries in the period from 1960 through 1970, mobility (rank shift) within this "Big 100" has decreased year by year and a more inflexible structure formed.

Now, based on an idea similar to that used by Dr. Utton in his tests carried out in the United Kingdom, and taking 69 sample industries selected at random from the approximately 260 industries covered by the *Oriental Economist* in its investigation of sales shares, I have tried to calculate the probability of the top 3 firms of each industry belonging to the "Big 200" firms (taken from the *President 500 Directory* and ranked by sales) in the mining and manufacturing industries. I found that in 83 percent of the 69 sample industries at least one of the top 3 firms belonged to the "Big 200" and the probability that the top 2 or 3 firms all belonged to the "Big 200" was approximately 70 percent. The average concentration ratio for industries in which the top 3 firms all belong to the "Big 200" was approximately 20 percent higher than the average concentration ratio for industries in which none of the top three firms belonged to the "Big 200." If we look at the results of these calculations, we find that an extremely close relationship exists between aggregate concentration and market concentration. Moreover, the six largest company groupings (even omitting financial institutions) account for approximately one-quarter of total assets, capital and sales of all industries. If we take all this into consideration, then in real terms a much higher level of concentration of economic power exists in Japan today than in the United States or Europe, and it must be said that in many markets, monopolistic companies, by creating various anticompetitive effects, have been causing the competitive market mechanism in the Japanese economy to decay.

On one occasion, Professor Fritz Machlup said before a public hearing of the U.S. Senate Committee on the Judiciary, Subcommittee on Antitrust and Monopoly, that "our Government has done much more to create monopoly than to destroy monopoly." It seems to me that this statement is perhaps more applicable to Japan than to the United States. Since its enactment in 1947, the Anti-Monopoly Law has been revised many times in the direction of alleviation (or rather deterioration). Now, almost 1,000 types of cartel (such as anti-depression cartels, rationalization cartels, export cartels, cartels for the protection of small and medium-sized firms, and so on) are recognized as exceptions to the law. Various forms of "gyosei-shido" (administrative guidance) which disregard the competitive price mechanism have played an important role in industrial and financial policy. And so on. And so on.

However, as I mentioned above, plans for strengthening Japan's Anti-Monopoly Law are at present (March 1975) under study and are expected to be presented to the Diet in the near future (see Appendix B). This is an epoch-making event in the history of anti-monopoly policy in Japan. The direction the following course of events will take is a matter of the greatest concern to us.

Appendix A: Proposed Main Points of the Anti-Monopoly Act Revision *

1. Partition of Enterprise

(1) If the Commission is of opinion that there exists a monopoly situation in any particular field of trade and that it is extremely difficult to restore competition by other means, the Commission may order the entrepreneur, for the purpose of remedying this situation, to divide his company or to transfer a part of his business.

(2) A monopoly situation means a situation meeting each of the following conditions.

    (i) The market share occupied by one or two companies is extremely high.[1]

    (ii) The competition is substantially restrained.

    (iii) A new entry to the particular field of trade concerned is extremely difficult.

(3) In issuing an order prescribed in Paragraph 1, the Commission shall give special consideration to the following items with respect to the entrepreneur concerned.

    (i) Capital, reserve and other aspects of the assets.

    (ii) Income and expenditure, and other aspects of operation.

    (iii) Location of factories, work yards, etc.

    (iv) Business facilities and equipment.

    (v) Technological features.

    (vi) Aspects of sales methods.

    (vii) Capacity for obtaining finance and materials.

    (viii) International competitivity.

    (ix) Others.

---

[1] 50 per cent by one company, 75 per cent by two companies.

* Source: Government of Japan, Fair Trade Commission, September 18, 1974.

(4)   The Commission may order the division of company as a remedy to a private monopolization.

2. *Disclosure of Cost*

(1)   If the Commission is of opinion that in an oligopolistic situation [2] the price is simultaneously raised as a result of concerted actions and that there exists no competition in price, the Commission may order the entrepreneur concerned to publish the cost of the product.

(2)   The entrepreneur who is ordered to publish the cost shall do so in conformity with the rule of calculation and the forms which will be provided by the Commission.

(3)   The categories of business and products subject to the publication of cost will be designated by the Commission.

3. *Rollback of Agreed Price*

(1)   In case the price is raised as a result of an unreasonable restraint of trade (hereinafter called "agreement"), the Commission may order the entrepreneur to restore the price level which existed before the agreement.

(2)   The order may indicate the period during which the price thus restored should be maintained not longer than six months, when the Commission thinks it necessary.

(3)   When the price raise is due to a marked degree of cost up not attributable to the responsibility of the entrepreneur, the Commission may take it into consideration.

(4)   The constituent entrepreneurs of the trade association who carried out a price raise as a result of decision of the association are subject to the same measure as prescribed above.

4. *Administrative Fine*

(1)   The Commission may impose an administrative fine on the entrepreneur who has unduly raised the price by an agreement.

(2)   The amount of the administrative fine is at maximum the difference between the agreed price and the original price, multiplied by the amount of sales carried out in the period covered by the agreement. For the purpose of this paragraph, this period is deemed to have ended at the time when the Commission decision is issued.

5. *Restriction on Stockholding by a Company*

(1)   Companies of a certain magnitude, engaging in other business than financing, are subject to the restriction under Paragraph 3 of this section.

---

[2] More than 70 per cent of the market share occupied by not more than 3 companies.

(2) A company of a certain magnitude means a company whose capital exceeds ten billion yen or whose gross assets exceed two hundred billion yen. Companies whose ratio of holding stock of other companies is extremely high are also subject to the restriction under Paragraph 3 of this section.

(3) A company falling within the category above-mentioned shall not hold stock of other domestic companies in excess of half the amount of its net assets or the amount of its capital, whichever larger.

(4) It is in principle prohibited for a company falling within the category above-mentioned to hold stock of another competing company in Japan. One can be exempted from this restriction by furnishing sufficient reasons under the Commission's approval.

(5) A reasonable period of deferment will be granted to a company, especially for the one who has to dispose a considerable amount of stock. This deferment period may be permitted to exceed five years, if necessary.

6. Restriction on Stockholding by a Financial Company

(1) No company engaging in financial business shall hold stock of another company in Japan in excess of 5 percent of the total outstanding stock of the latter.

(2) An appropriate period of deferment shall be granted to a financial company, according to the amount of stock it disposes.

7. Penal Provisions

(1) The upper limit of the fine (actually 500,000 yen) shall be raised at least to 5,000,000 yen.

(2) Any director representing a corporation, who, knowing that a violation is planned, fails to take the necessary steps to prevent it or who, knowing of the violation, fails to take the necessary steps to remedy it, shall be liable to a fine.

8. Unfair Business Practices

(1) Measures against unfair business practices are to be amended so that measures taken against violations of Section 3 (Private Monopolization and Unreasonable Restraint of Trade) may be applied *mutatis mutandis.*

(2) Penal punishments will be applied to unfair business practices although this is actually not the case.

9. Measures against a Past Violation

Actually no measure can be taken under the provisions of the Act against a violation already terminated. The Act will be amended so that appropriate measures may be taken against a past violation in order to prevent a repetition of the violation.

Appendix B: Government Plan to Revise the Anti-Monopoly Law *

1. Administrative Fine

(1) As an administrative measure to assure the effectiveness of "illegal cartel prohibition" provision, the Fair Trade Commission (FTC) would be empowered to order payment of administrative fines on excess profits obtained through illegal cartel practices.

(2) The amount of the administrative fine would be the difference between the profit per unit of the product in the profitable period and that in a certain period previous to the agreement, multiplied by the amount of sales carried out in the period covered by the agreement. The method of calculation is to be provided by government ordinance.

(3) The provision would also apply to the associations of producers that supported illegal acts.

(4) The related provisions such as "not to be counted in business expenses" in computing the income in tax accounting and procedures such as compulsory collection procedures would be revised.

2. Penal Provisions

The maximum of fine would be raised from ¥500,000 at present to an amount yet to be determined. Penalties would be levied on representatives of the corporations that formed illegal cartels.

3. Enforcement of Prohibition Measures of Illegal Cartels

(1) To assure the measure to eliminate illegal cartels (unreasonable restraint of trade), the FTC would order corporations to take specific actions concerning price and other business practices, to report thereof to the said commission, and also to report on actions taken after dissolution of cartel agreement.

(2) The provision would also apply to the associations of producers that supported illegal acts.

4. Reports on Collusive Price Increase

(1) In a highly oligopolistic industry, where all leading firms raised prices almost the same amounts or ratio in a certain period, the FTC would order them to report the reason for the price increases.

(2) The FTC must publish in its annual report to the Diet the summary of the reasons for price increases reported by each firm as well as the FTC comment thereon.

---

* Unofficial and tentative translation, March 5, 1975.

5. *Business Divestiture*

(1) Where there exists a monopolistic situation in any particular field of trade and it is extremely difficult to restore competition by any other means, the FTC may order the firm, for the purpose of remedying this situation and eliminating a monopolistic situation and restoring competition, to transfer a part of its business (including investment capital assets and/or shares) and to take other necessary measures. But these measures are not to apply to such cases where it is clear that they would have a strong adverse effect on economies of scale, financial soundness or the international competitive position of the firm.

(2) A monopolistic situation means a situation meeting each of the following conditions:

(i) The market share occupied by one or two companies is extremely high (minimum share would be 50 percent if only one firm was involved, and 75 percent if two firms were involved).

(ii) New entries into a given industry are restricted to such an extent that it is extremely difficult to start new businesses.

(iii) Competition is substantively restricted, as shown by the following two conditions: (a) prices fixed for a long period of time without reflecting production costs or supply-demand relations, and (b) exceedingly high profit rates or exceedingly high rates of expenditure prevailing over a long period of time.

(3) In issuing an order prescribed in paragraph (1), the FTC should make an effort to limit transfer of operations to an extent needed to eliminate the monopolistic situation and to restore competition and take deliberate care not to disturb the business of corporations concerned and related corporations or livelihood of employees.

In so doing, the FTC shall give special consideration to the following items with respect to the firm concerned:

(i) Assets, income and expenditure and other aspects of operation,

(ii) Aspects of officers and employees,

(iii) Location of factories and work yards,

(iv) Business facilities and equipment,

(v) Existence, contents and technological features of industrial property rights,

(vi) Capacity and actual state of production and sales,

(vii) Capacity for obtaining finance and materials and their actual state,

(viii) The actual state of production and distribution of the same or similar commodity.

(4) In the case in which the transfer order written in paragraph (1) is issued, the FTC would beforehand consult with the Cabinet ministers concerned.

(5) The provisions with regard to procedures of holding a public hearing and other items would be arranged.

6. *Restriction on Stockholding by a Company*

(1) Except for financial institutions, a large scale business corporation (with a capital of ¥10,000 million or more, or net assets of ¥30,000 million or more, which criteria will be decided by the government ordinance in the future) will not be allowed to hold shares of other domestic firms in excess of either its capital or net assets, whichever is larger at the end of each business year.

(2) For ten years during a transition period, where shares held on the effective date of this revision are beyond the limitation shown in paragraph (1), the former figure will be the maximum (where the amount of shares held at the end of 1974 is below that amount, the higher figure will be used). The obtaining of new shares of increased capital stock will be allowed in a certain period.

(3) This provision would not apply to the following items:

(i) (a) Shares of corporations in which the central government or local organization hold an interest, and (b) shares of firms which require very large investment funds and must conduct operations involving high risks, or companies whose activities are regarded by the government ordinance as highly important to the national economy.

(ii) Shares of corporations which carry out their operations only abroad and those of corporations which only invest or give financial facilities of long term to such corporations.

(iii) Shares held as the result of the enforcement of liens, pledges, mortgages, or of payment in kind, which obtain the approval of FTC (in a certain period).

(iv) Ownership of shares of a wholly owned subsidiary which is established to carry out a part of business (in a certain period).

THE THREAT FROM
THE EMERGENCE OF CARTELS AND
MONOPOLY POWER

M. A. Adelman

Any discussion of world monopoly must of course be dominated by the greatest monopoly of all time, the cartel of the OPEC nations (but not OPEC itself), whose annual tribute is $100 billion per year. Few cartels have ever collected even 1 percent of that.

Since current prices and revenues are the work of a monopoly, it follows that the burden of supporting them is unnecessary. Absent the monopoly, price would be at a very small fraction of its current level, because oil is plentiful. Of course the Club of Rome nonsense has bitten deep. The world shortage of raw materials is a fiction, but belief in the fiction is a fact. Not scarcity, but the belief in scarcity by the consuming governments and most public opinion explains the oil price explosion. Nevertheless, it should be emphasized that the fear of imminent raw material exhaustion has for its basis a complete disregard of theory, statistics, and history. Everything that is said today about mineral exhaustion was said much better in 1865 by the English economist Stanley Jevons, who warned of the approaching exhaustion of coal. The first year for which we have world oil reserve statistics, such as they are, was 1938, when production was 6 percent of reserves, compared to 3 percent last year.

There has been no long-run tendency for minerals prices to rise—some have risen, some have fallen, and some have done both or neither. The history of prices is particularly important because the price at any moment reflects supply and demand not only at the moment but also for the future. The expectation of a price rise makes holders of mineral bodies hold back on development investment, for the sake of greater profits in the future. This raises costs and prices. Up to the middle of 1970, there was no tendency for oil prices to rise—quite the contrary. Furthermore, long-term contracts were being signed at lower prices than spot contracts, showing that the price was expected to keep decreasing.

There is a feeling of guilt in the developed countries over having supposedly exploited the raw material producers of the less developed countries. Prices are said to have been "too low," an indisputable statement because nobody has explained what "too low" means. It certainly cannot mean too low to equate demand with supply, since there was always a potential surplus in the world oil trade—a potential surplus which now and again broke into actuality and today is gigantic.

Despite the long-time decline in oil prices, which amounted to about 65 percent in real terms between World War II and 1970, there was a flow of billions of dollars into the industry, and no shortage of investment. If there were anything in the theory that higher demand or deficient supply sent up the price of oil, then huge excessive capacity in 1974 should have sent it down. Secretary Kissinger said in December 1973 that the problem was a surge of demand against insufficient inducements to invest. This delusion helps to explain why prices rose an additional 50 percent in 1975.

Every monopoly is to a large extent a learning process, a finding out how much one can get away with, and the oil cartel learned many profitable lessons between 1970 and 1973. The cartel can be understood as largely an economic phenomenon. True, Mr. Kissinger thinks that current oil prices are explained by "political factors," and hopes to bring them down by political arrangements. But this is nonsense. A group of sellers who raise the price and increase their revenues thereby is acting like rational men: we need no special political explanation for their actions. The oil-producing nations have widely disparate interests. Some 40 percent of producing capacity is non-Arab, and among the Arabs there are important dissensions. In any case, all this is secondary. What really matters is that there is no opposition between economic and political goals, no need to sacrifice one for the other. Money is power, and the more money these nations have, the greater their weight in world affairs generally and on their own borders particularly. The same is of course true for all other raw-material cartels.

So much for the origin of the problem. What of its impact on our two countries? During the past year I have more than once had to caution an audience that they must be a little wary in listening to me because the world oil monopoly was a misfortune for my country, but a piece of great good fortune for them, good fortune which they should exploit as best they can. In this instance, there is no such caution, because the cartel has been a misfortune for both Japan and the United States.

Of course, some Americans and some Japanese will get rich working on export orders, contracts, and so on. But the value of these is insignificant compared even with the direct economic burden, the billions of dollars paid out in high prices. And it should be noted that the burden on the United States is really not much less than the burden on Japan, although we have a large domestic energy industry. Americans are now being forced to divert capital and labor from areas where they could be used more productively into providing domestic energy at very high cost. Domestic energy makes it easier to manage the balance of payments, but that is a problem which is already seen as much less important than it was even a few months ago.

56

The second ill consequence for our countries is that much of the oil exporters' revenues will not be spent on imports. The importing countries therefore cannot pay for oil in exports and must run a deficit—a deficit which last year was about $55 billion. Every importing nation would like to avoid going into debt for its oil supplies—not to mention the possibility of strategic industries being taken over by foreigners, possibly hostile ones. Hence consuming countries are strenuously trying to promote exports and limit imports, through "beggar-my-neighbor" commercial policies. We risk drifting back to the disastrous commercial rivalry of the 1930s, though, as *The Economist* said, it "is to the credit of (nearly all) industrialized countries that they have, by and large, adhered to their pledge that they took nearly a year ago not to go in for mutual beggar-my-neighbor." [1]

The accumulation of the oil producers' surpluses will apparently not be as quick or as massive as was feared at first. Instead of about $650 billion by 1980, apparently it will be between $180 billion (Morgan Guaranty) and $460 billion (World Bank). How much difference this makes we cannot as yet say, but there is no doubt the surpluses will have a destabilizing effect on world capital markets and on world politics.

The surplus problem appears less acute than was expected because the oil-exporting nations have increased their imports much faster than anyone believed they would. Their imports were up last year by 75 percent, and to the astonishment of many, some of the richest nations, most notably Abu Dhabi and Qatar, have succeeded in spending even more than they have received and are in financial trouble—trouble which, to be sure, is curable without much difficulty. The consensus appears to be that this surge in imports cannot continue. But there is one import which has just begun and which is far more likely to be expanded than any other, and that is armaments.

This brings me to the third effect, which is the arms race in the Persian Gulf and elsewhere. The current sky-high oil price means that every little patch of barren ground or salt water that may possibly have oil underneath is worth fighting for, and of course the oil revenues provide the means for the fighting. Greece and Turkey were already squaring off when the quarrel erupted over Cyprus. The mere possibility of large oil deposits in the East China Sea has increased tension there.

I cannot tell how long it will be before one of the oil-exporting nations has nuclear weapons. India spent only about $175 million to develop its atomic capability. Since none of the oil exporters has a comparably trained technical force, perhaps it would take them a billion dollars; the question is only how many will have nuclear weapons how soon? Billions of dollars are coming into the hands of reckless men who are willing to set the world on fire. A few short years ago Libya was "a nice, safe, conservative pro-Western monarchy, a good place to do business"—very much like Saudi Arabia, the super-Libya of the future.

---

[1] April 5, 1975, p. 68.

And hardly a year ago Libya could at least be trusted to denounce the Soviet Union; that too has changed. Saudi Arabia may use the arms and training provided by my government to invade and occupy its neighbors' oil fields to suppress their competition, as a sensible monopolist should. Iran is more likely to control the Strait of Hormuz, the cork in the Persian Gulf bottle. This will soon be practical. International law and contracts are severely diminished. The Caracas conference on a law of the sea failed, because the control over the seabed is worth too much for anybody to sign away any possible claim he has on it.

Investment in minerals in the less developed countries will now decrease as they follow the example of the OPEC nations, both in takeovers and in trying to form cartels. The chances are good that some will raise prices above competitive levels, at least for a time. But none can hope for more than a faint imitation of the oil cartel's success, because none can hope so to frighten the consuming countries out of their wits. In the long run these new cartels will mostly or all fail, because no product approaches oil in its lack of substitutes, high cost of storage, and—perhaps most important—its perishability. Most minerals, especially the essential ones, take the form of durable goods and are used over a period of many years. If the industrial nations were suddenly deprived of any new copper, tin, lead, zinc, or aluminum, the only effect would be on employment. They could do without perfectly well for a long enough time to embarrass or ruin most of the producing countries. The less developed countries who try to imitate OPEC will lose investment, which will move instead to the developed areas. This is wasteful, since costs will be higher, but safety of investment will require it. Everybody will lose, just as is happening in oil.

For those less developed countries which do not draw large revenues from raw materials, the oil cartel and other cartels are of course a worse disaster than for the developed countries. Thousands or millions will die directly of starvation or of disease because of the impossibility of paying for oil exports. One would never know this by listening to the governments of the fourth world. In part, ideology overcomes self-interest; moreover, these governments need favors, and must pay for them in flattery and support.

The next unfortunate effect on Japan, the United States, and other developed countries is the kind of dissension seen during the Arab production cutback of 1973–1974. As a boycott or embargo it was completely ineffective. As some predicted, there was an exchange of customers, with non-Arab oil going to the United States. The Arabs alone come out of this unfortunate affair with credit. They were bold, not rash, and did not overplay their hand. Their reduction in output was quite moderate and though it increased prices enormously, it never threatened any large-scale shutdown anywhere. Had they stopped producing altogether, there would have been a swift military reaction from Europe and Asia, probably with the United States leading the way by the universal request of the oil-consuming nations. Instead, the Arabs achieved a great result with little risk or danger to themselves. The nations of the European Community broke their own law, the Treaty of Rome, which forbids interference with the movement of goods between any community nations, when they prevented oil reshipments to the Netherlands. Japan had been as cooperative with the Arabs as any other nation, the minister of trade and industry having warned in early 1973 that Japan would have no part of any action which even seemed to be directed against the oil-producing nations. Far from cooperation helping Japan, it wound up with Japan's being put on the list of nonfriendly nations. By letting themselves be pushed, the Japanese had demonstrated that it was profitable to push them.

As for the United States, our government was and is obsessed with the notion that we must do nothing to resist. Our ambassador to Saudi Arabia was permitted to urge American citizens to pressure our own government to agree to Arab demands: he made wildly untrue statements to panic public opinion in the United States. American oil companies, the participants in the Arabian-American Oil Company (ARAMCO), acted with the knowledge and consent of our government as the agents of Saudi Arabia on foreign soil, to administer a boycott which Saudi Arabia had not the personnel and facilities to administer.

By earning the contempt of Saudi Arabia, my government set the stage for the extraordinary events of 1974, when Saudi Arabia repeatedly claimed to be trying to bring prices down, was applauded for this by the United States, and then raised prices. From the end of 1973 through early November 1974, the basic price at the Persian Gulf, the government take (compared to which the company margin is negligible), rose by not quite 50 percent, from $7.00 to about $10.25. Saudi Arabia was the price leader of each increase, Iran being only the follower.

The road to this disaster, and its threat to economic and political order, is plain—"dialogue" with the producing countries, or "cooperation, not confrontation." The talk of force only shows the poverty of the ideas of the consuming countries, and this poverty is the reason for our troubles. There is apparently a complete inability on our part to look at a cartel as a problem in economic policy. It is only considered as political, to be solved by negotiation, and by force if nothing else works.

We have been permitted to see very little of what actually happened these last five years. There is just a glimpse of it in what we know of the meetings in Washington in 1970, when the oil companies and the U.S. government conferred on the Libyan demands. At least one oil company knew that capitulation was even more dangerous than resistance. Some companies agreed, some disagreed, some waffled, but the United States government was firmly against any resistance. Then as at Tehran six months later, and ever since then, United States policy has been well summed up by Mr. George Meany in the one word—pay.

The United States government is now trying to freeze a dismal present into the indefinite future by having the consuming governments commit themselves to a long-term floor under the international oil market. This, if it is carried out, promises the cartel long life and threatens to multiply the disasters flowing from it.

The very idea of a long-term contract with a sovereign monopolist is absurd. A contract is enforced by law and by competition: if one of the parties does not keep his word, perhaps others can be found who will. But the oil cartel, like the other raw materials cartels, is composed of sovereign states to whom no law applies. The producing governments have never kept one of the many agreements they have signed. In 1973, Sheikh Yamani, the petroleum minister of Saudi Arabia, stated that the government "in Saudi Arabia would have liked to abide by and honor the Tehran agreements, but . . ." circumstances had changed. At a meeting sponsored by the American Enterprise Institute last October, Sheikh Yamani pledged not to reduce output. Saudi Arabia has in fact reduced output, from over 9 to 6.5 million barrels daily, and American officials have complained that the broken word "pulled the rug from under them." [2] But the lesson has been lost on my government. If Mr. Kissinger succeeds in his grand design for a world price-fixing agreement, some day Sheikh Yamani will, if convenient, say that he and his colleagues would have dearly loved to honor the agreement, but circumstances . . . and so on.

For the United States and for Japan the moral is simple: better to do nothing than to do harm. Stop cooperating with the exporting countries and take counsel on how to get rid of an unnecessary economic and political burden. All cartels have broken down in the past because of excess capacity. This cartel is now carrying an enormous burden of excess capacity, about one-third of total capacity by mid-1975. It is carrying the burden successfully because of two protections. First, the multinational companies are a vehicle to fix prices, limit output, and divide markets, without any collusion. The companies sell as much as they can at current prices and produce only what they can sell. This rather haphazard allocation among the producing countries is worse for some than for others, but so long as they are prepared to accept the burden, the cartel is in good shape. The second support for the cartel lies in the ability of a few countries, most notably Saudi Arabia and some of the other sparsely populated nations, to tolerate deep cutbacks. They can, if need be, let the other countries produce to the limit, knowing those limits are quickly reached, and thereby accept the whole burden of reduction. But at this moment, and probably for another year, the "price makers" cannot do this. Right now, if all of the countries except Saudi Arabia produced at full capacity, that country could shut down completely and production would still be equal to the amount demanded. Of course Saudi Arabia would not tolerate this; in fact will not even tolerate any very large reduction. Therefore, if the

---

[2] *Oil and Gas Journal*, March 17, 1975.

others do not hold back, Saudi Arabia must retaliate, which would speedily crack the cartel. Hence the strategy for the consuming countries is simple: promote competition among the producing countries, approach them with offers of large additional sales at lower prices, and leave Saudi Arabia and similar countries to cut back output as much as possible.

This will not kill the cartel overnight, and even when there is a breakdown the cartel will be rebuilt. The rewards of this colossal raid have been so enormous that its memory will endure for a long time, and producers of other raw materials will try to emulate the OPEC cartel. I have suggested elsewhere (in hearings, as yet unpublished, of the Senate Foreign Relations Committee, Subcommittee on Multinational Corporations) a tactic for the United States to follow, which by the way was suggested to me by a Japanese policy years ago. Whatever the tactic, the time to change strategy, to resist current evils and ward off worse ones is right now. There should be no agreement with any cartel; the International Energy Agency should be strictly confined to crisis management; the efforts at a world price-fixing agreement should be repudiated.

COMMENTARY

Edward J. Mitchell

I feel at a disadvantage in discussing these papers. My disadvantage in discussing Professor Baba's paper is that I know almost nothing about Japanese industry, so that I must resort to asking questions about his paper rather than making positive comments. My disadvantage in discussing Professor Adelman's paper is that I agree with him on just about everything he has said, and I find that useful discussions are better based on disagreements than on agreements.

Let me begin with Professor Baba's paper. He focuses on the question of concentration in Japanese industry. I raise the question how important the concentration of industry (at the levels we are talking about) is with regard to competition. As you may know, there have been a number of studies in the United States attempting to discover the importance of concentration in determining whether industries are competitive, or whether concentration means monopoly pricing or monopoly profits, and so on. As I read these studies, it seems that concentration may not be as important as was imagined earlier. I wonder whether any studies have been done in Japan to see whether concentrated industries are more profitable than unconcentrated industries, and whether industries that are becoming more concentrated find that their profits increase with increased concentration. I also wonder whether the concentration data Professor Baba is using in his study apply to domestic production, or whether they represent the domestic firm's share of the whole market—which raises the whole question of imports as a method of introducing competition.

I wonder also about the extent to which the developing concentration and any excess profits that might exist are the result of an absence of competition from abroad. Just one comment on this from my own research in the U.S. oil industry: I would make a guess—it is not something that one could prove and Professor Adelman may want to disagree with me—that if the U.S. oil industry became significantly more concentrated, let us say if the number of large companies fell from twenty to ten and the number of independent oil companies also fell by half, the industry would not become significantly less competitive, if "competition" means price taking and "monopoly" means the ability to set discretionary prices in the marketplace.

Turning to Professor Adelman's paper, I repeat that he and I do not have any significant disagreements, so I will just go over the agreements quickly. Dr. Bergsten has assured us that he will raise some new disagreements about which we can all argue hereafter. In any case, I agree with Professor Adelman that scarcity is not the problem. But I would add that the expectation on the part of some governments that prices may be higher in the future—that is, the belief, not on the part of industry but on the part of some governments, that oil is really scarce and becoming more scarce—must help to keep prices up. For example, it may be possible to interpret Canadian government policy or Venezuelan policy on this basis, so that this expectational phenomenon would in fact be helping to support the cartel.

I would like to elaborate on Professor Adelman's point that the cartel is not doomed to collapse, as many economists who do not study the oil market seem to believe. Their instinctive belief is that cartels will all disappear within a few years and that this one cannot be an exception. But if one looks at scenarios as to what might happen with this cartel, it seems to me likely that the key members of the cartel might over time be induced to charge lower prices to maintain the cartel, rather than attempting to maintain the kind of prices that exist now, if the attempt to keep current prices might allow the whole thing to fall apart. The reason I suggest this is that if the cartel fell apart completely— that is, if there were competition among all its members—the price would plummet precipitously. I cannot imagine such members of the cartel as Saudi Arabia allowing that to happen, and I think they could prevent that from happening.

I agree with Professor Adelman's view that successful imitation of the cartel is unlikely; that oil is unique; that the opportunities for having cartels in other commodities have existed all along. Such cartels have been attempted and they have failed. I see a special situation in oil that arose in the latter part of the 1960s and the early 1970s. I am not familiar with all the other commodity markets, but I do not see situations of the same nature arising in the other markets.

Finally, I would like to discuss what it is that we should do about this. Professor Adelman has suggested some remedies, and I would like to make two additional points. First, I think that neither the United States nor Japan should subsidize OPEC. I do not know precisely what Japanese oil policy is, but in the United States we do subsidize OPEC. We do not let the domestic price of energy in various submarkets reflect the world price. We keep the domestic price down, and in that way, when someone goes in and buys a gallon of gasoline, if it is an OPEC gallon, he winds up paying less than what the United States is effectively paying OPEC for that oil. And if it is an American gallon, he winds up paying more than what the American producer effectively receives for that gallon. In that way domestic producers subsidize OPEC.

I also agree with Professor Adelman that we should not negotiate with OPEC. We should negotiate, however, with individual members of OPEC to lower the price. I hoped that Professor Adelman would mention the proposal to use quotas as a method of reducing prices of imported oil by having quotas and sealed bid auctions. I disagree with that proposal, but I do not disagree with the idea of using the federal government to negotiate lower prices with foreign governments so long as we do not install quotas.

I think my problem with the quota and sealed bid auction is simply that Professor Adelman would not be running it. If he did, I think I might approve of it. I have some experience with quotas in the government, and I know what in fact will be done with them and it will not be what I—or he—would desire.

C. Fred Bergsten

I want to comment first on points in Professor Baba's paper, then make a few comments on oil in relation to Professor Adelman's presentation, and then perhaps try to engineer a little controversy by taking a somewhat different line on the probability of success of other cartels that might emulate OPEC in other primary products.

To Professor Baba's paper I would simply add two points that relate international economic events to the trend of cartelization he sees in Japanese industry. It would seem to me that the outside world has reinforced the trend toward cartelization in Japan by foisting on Japanese industry the so-called "voluntary export restraints" in a number of specific industries. It is pretty clear that the United States, after having gone to great lengths to try to break up "zaibatsu," turned around ten years later and started creating one in the textile industry, which had been competitive in Japan into the middle 1950s. But then, when the United States required the Japanese to allocate among themselves the exports that could be made to the United States, the Japanese textile industry obviously had to organize itself to allocate those export quotas. This sequence of events created the potential for a much greater degree of administered price power than had previously existed in that particular market.[1]

The U.S. effort on steel, which began in 1968 and has just now expired, had a similar impact. There, however, the industry was already highly concentrated, and the "voluntary restraints" gave the concentration an added fillip. And there are a number of minor industries in which U.S. and European pressure

---

[1] For a comprehensive analysis, see C. Fred Bergsten, "On the Non-Equivalence of Import Quotas and 'Voluntary' Export Restraints" in Bergsten, ed., *Toward A New World Trade Policy: The Maidenhead Papers* (Lexington, Mass.: Heath-Lexington Books, 1975), also Brookings Reprint T-009.

for voluntary export restraints have either created or at least pushed much further the tendency of Japanese industry to cartelize internally. I would be interested in seeing, in any further extension of the work that Professor Baba or his colleagues may do in Japan, an effort to isolate this element and see how much of Japan's cartelization could legitimately be blamed on the outside world.

My second point is to raise a question about the impact of international investment on industrial concentration in Japan. Some of the work we are doing at Brookings suggests that the expansion of foreign investment by American firms has significantly added to their market power within the United States. The point is not simply that there are common causal factors that promote both domestic market concentration and foreign investment, but rather that the foreign investment variable per se shows up as a significant factor adding to the market power of firms within the United States.

I am curious whether the increased multinationalization of Japanese firms that has taken place in the last five years or so might be having a similar impact in Japan. It may now be the case that there does exist a correlation at the most superficial level: the recent increase in concentration that Professor Baba points to in Japan does coincide in time with the first expansion of international investment by Japanese firms. I wonder whether there might be some causal effect there as well.

A related point is that Japan's resistance to incoming foreign investment, as well as to incoming imports, may have made it easier for Japanese firms to tie up their domestic market. I do not mean to suggest that letting foreign firms into a country necessarily reduces industrial concentration. In some cases, it may add to concentration. But in the case of a strong economy such as Japan's, with many capable independent firms, permitting foreign investment to come into Japan as well as relaxing import barriers might be helpful in fighting the trend toward concentration that Professor Baba sees. Thus, in any extension of this analysis, I think it would be interesting to look at the impact of both outward and inward foreign direct investment on concentration trends in Japan, and to consider inward investment along with increased import flows as measures that might help cope with the problem that he sees.

Turning now to oil, I, like Dr. Mitchell, agree with much of what Professor Adelman has said. But there are two or three points where I would disagree. One is Professor Adelman's stress on the "beggar-thy-neighbor" policies that he sees the oil-consuming countries carrying out in trying to avoid current account deficits from the shift in oil prices.

I would rather agree with what Professor Cooper said in his final comment: that when we look at the extent of the oil shock, particularly with the contact of a world of rampant inflation and now galloping recession, I think we have to come away encouraged by the relative absence of that kind of policy. It is true that, around the margin, one sees Australia, Finland, and perhaps a few other middle-sized countries now beginning to resort to some import restrictions. However, these have been adopted primarily for domestic employment reasons, not balance-of-payments reasons.

There has been the charge of a major Japanese export drive. I frankly do not see anything wrong with the Japanese going out and working hard to try to sell more goods abroad. If they were to adopt high government subsidies and competitive depreciation of the yen, then there would be something wrong. But I have not seen either of those steps being taken. I may have missed something, but I have not seen Japan—or in fact any other major country—competitively depreciating its exchange rate. Indeed, because of the concern with inflationary effects, countries over the past two or three years have wanted to avoid depreciation of their exchange rates. So I would be a good bit more sanguine than Professor Adelman about the willingness of the oil-consuming countries to resist the temptation to turn to "beggar-thy-neighbor" policies and try to export the problems caused for them by the oil crisis.

A second point on which I would differ with Professor Adelman relates to his admiration for how skillful OPEC was in pulling off the embargo and price increase. He is quite right that OPEC did not go so far as to trigger invasion. But from the standpoint of a maximizing oligopolist in economic terms, they did push the price up too far too fast. By doing so, they triggered responses from the consuming countries greater than would have occurred had they ratcheted the price up less rapidly than they did.

Only the drastic extent of the price rise triggered a Project Independence in this country and similar efforts elsewhere. In addition, purely in market terms, there are real nonlinearities in the price elasticities of demand. For oil consumers may not respond very much to a 20 percent, 30 percent, or even 50 percent change in price, but they do when the price rises fivefold. American business, particularly, has adopted a wave of programs to rationalize its energy consumption, leading to cutbacks in the consumption level. I would hypothesize—though I obviously cannot prove it—that this sequence of events might lead over the longer run to a weaker market for oil than OPEC might have triggered had its prices been raised more slowly over time.

I hasten to say that, even if prices were to drop back to $6 or $7 a barrel, OPEC would still be by far the most successful oligopoly in history. I do not mean to say that it is going to fail, or fall apart, but, at the same time, it does seem that, because OPEC pushed too far too fast, we now have significant downward pressure on the price of oil. Indeed, the real price is already down, simply because the nominal price has not risen as much in the last nine months as have inflation rates in general. The depreciation of the dollar, in which oil payments are mainly denominated, has of course reduced oil prices further. There have been significant cutbacks in the nominal prices of so-called "premium grade crudes." There have been longer extensions of credit by the OPEC countries, again reducing the real price to the buyers. And some of the oil-producing countries, notably Venezuela and Nigeria, are extending cut-rate sales to a number of their clients in Latin America and Africa, respectively.

I would not even be surprised if OPEC started offering cash rebates. That is what most sellers are doing in this recessionary market. They want to hold their posted price, whether it is Sunbeam appliances or Ford Pintos, but they will give us cash rebates. Abu Dhabi apparently offered one to the Japanese, a 5 percent discounted price for a long-term contract, but the Japanese turned it down—in my view, quite astutely. So there is already a significant decline in the real price of oil, and all indications suggest that the decline will go a good bit further. This really verifies what Dr. Mitchell was suggesting a minute ago: that Saudi Arabia, particularly, would take steps to cut the oil price in real terms to avoid major pressure that might break up the cartel.

As one piece of evidence, I would point to the fact that the Saudis and the other OPEC countries know that the depreciation of the dollar is reducing their real price. An obvious question is thus why, despite all their talk about it, they have not changed the denomination of their oil exports from dollars to SDRs or Deutschemarks or something else. In my view, their failure to do so can be at least partly explained by the fact that the depreciation of the dollar is helping them. It provides a cover for the erosion of the real price without their having to admit that the nominal posted price has to come down. So the depreciation of the dollar, and the reduction in real oil prices that it triggers, is in fact useful in this weak oil market to enable the OPEC cartel to maintain to the world that there has been no change in the posted price, therefore maintaining the illusion that the cartel is holding fast right where it was as long as nine months ago.

There is in fact only one force in the world right now for higher oil prices: the United States government. Our government fully agrees with what Professor Adelman said. Indeed U.S. oil policy is being determined wholly by perceptions— in my view, misperceptions—of foreign policy advantages, relating to short-term negotiating positions in the Middle East and long-term restoration of U.S. hegemony among its allies. I think these are internally inconsistent and erroneous policies, but they are after all being pushed by people who do not understand much about economics. Parenthetically, I very much liked Professor Adelman's polemic in his paper about Mr. Kissinger's inadequacies as a macroeconomist.

There are measures that have to be taken, I think, to deal with the vulnerability of the United States and Japan and other consuming countries to a possible cutoff of oil in the future. But the way to deal with this vulnerability is through joint stockpiles, the defensive kind of sharing arrangements we now have in the International Energy Agency (IEA) and, over the longer run, contracts with companies to develop new sources of energy and bring them on-stream, rather than through floor prices which could keep the cost of energy far too high for the future.

Indeed, policies of this sort bring me directly to the topic of this conference. I think they could be very dangerous to international relationships between the United States and Japan and among other consuming countries. We have already seen, in the IEA, quite a lot of conflict over whether to have a floor price and, if so, the level at which it should rest. Now if the United States were to adopt a floor price higher than the floor price (if any) adopted by Japan, two kinds of difficulties would be possible.

One would be in the economic security the United States would be buying. Japan would be jealous and, in a crisis, the United States would come out well. Japan would be in even more of a supplicant's position than it was last time. But, in the ongoing period when there was no crisis, the shoe would be on the other foot. If the United States were to condemn itself to high costs for energy inputs, whereas Japan continued to take advantage of lower-cost world oil, the United States would suffer competitively and the dollar would depreciate. Back would come the same kinds of pressures for import protectionism and charges against excessive Japanese competitiveness that we heard in the late 1960s and early 1970s—and which played a major role in providing the crisis that destroyed the Bretton Woods monetary system. So unless international agreement could be reached on a floor price and indeed on common across-the-board oil policy, I think there would be real sources of conflict between Japan and the United States, sources of conflict which would be very dangerous for our overall relationship.

Finally, turning to the question of other cartels, I would say immediately that none of the others would be even in the ballpark with the oil cartel in quantitative impact. There is no question on that score. Oil is incomparably more important than any other materials subject to cartels in quantitative and political terms. I would also agree that the Club of Rome stuff is nonsense; there is no outlook for physical shortages in any of the raw materials that we are talking about in the foreseeable future. But everyone now agrees that the developing countries, and other primary producing countries including Canada and Australia, are going to try their hand at the same game. We now have functioning commodity cartels or cartel-like arrangements in at least ten primary products: oil, bauxite, copper, coffee, phosphates, bananas, rubber and, just recently, mercury, manganese and iron ore.

To be sure, these efforts are having different degrees of success so far. If we cyclically adjust the commodity markets for the current deep recession, however, we will find that prices across the board are a good bit higher than anyone would have expected. If we look at the indices for all commodities, be they for foodstuffs or industrial raw materials, and compare them with what one would have expected in the face of negative growth in the United States and Japan and some other countries, in both 1974 and 1975, those prices do not look low at all. The bauxite price has stayed way up as has the oil price, in the face of the recession. In response to the 15 percent production cutbacks by CIPEC countries, the copper price has bounced back 20 percent from its low of two months ago. How much one wants to attribute this price move to the cartel action, and how much to market events, is always conjectural. But even in copper, the picture is simply not one of a cartel that has not had any effect.

In my view, some of the cartels can work and probably have significant effects, at least over the medium term. The work that has been done on price elasticities of both supply and demand is not good for most of these commodity markets. But, to the extent we have the figures, it looks like those elasticities are pretty low, not just in the short term but also in the medium term—well under unity for most of the raw materials on which studies have been done: 0.5 for example for tin; 0.4 for copper or aluminum, even over periods of five years or more.

It is also clear that the supply functions are nonlinear for most of these products. It takes massive investments to get new output on line. A copper mine takes six or seven years to bring on-stream. Political instability in most of the countries where such investment would take place reduces the propensity of private firms to make the kinds of investments that most of us, as economists, assume would occur in response to price cartelization efforts.

Indeed, in a number of industries there is the same support for the producing countries' cartel from the multinational firms that there is in oil. Aluminum is very much in a similar situation, where the multinational aluminum companies have the same interest in promoting the cartel as the international oil companies have in collaborating with OPEC.

Dr. Mitchell asked what has changed. I think a number of things have changed, and believe that cartels will be tried even for commodities where they did not work in the past. One reason is that OPEC itself did work, demonstrating not only that producers can get together but that consumers cannot get together. One of the fears in trying to cartelize in the past was that the consumers would get together and simply mow the producers down, in economic terms. But in oil they scrambled every which way. There has been no reaction to the efforts in bauxite. The producing countries have taken heart.

Another change—and Professor Adelman referred to this quite clearly—is in the politics of the situation. It has now become the key indicator of third world *machismo* to try your own commodity cartel. If you do not, it becomes hard for you to stand up at UNCTAD or UNIDO or anywhere else; your colleagues are trying the game, so you have to try, because of third world politics.

We all know how serious the developing countries are about creating what they call a "new international economic order." It is clear that commodity power is the leading wedge in pursuing that objective. The third world countries are going to pursue it as much as they can. Indeed, that objective may submerge some of the differences that might otherwise exist among the producing countries, in pure market share calculations, and enable them to succeed in cases where they did not in the past.

Professor Adelman has suggested that the other cartels will not succeed because consumers could do without their products. I am skeptical of that conclusion. At the margin, it would be very hard for the United States to say it would do without aluminum, tin, copper, or some of these other materials. Technically it could be done, but the price would be high. Here it seems it would be much easier to capitulate. That is what the United States has done in bauxite and what it will probably do in other materials, enabling the other cartels to do well as long as they do not emulate OPEC's one mistake, which was to push too far too fast. And the others may have learned from OPEC that it is not wise to do that, thereby increasing their chances for success.

They have also learned how to play the public relations game a bit better than OPEC and the oil companies. The aluminum companies scream all the way to the bank as they benefit from the price rises in bauxite in Jamaica. They have learned, unlike the oil companies, to scream, go to international arbitration, take out ads in the papers to oppose the action—all the way to the bank. So I think that, on the side of public reactions, OPEC has also taught some lessons to its emulators.

Putting all this together, in both economic and political terms, I believe not only that there is a strong likelihood that the other cartel efforts will be tried, but that there are strong reasons to think they will succeed. The cartels are indeed looking fairly successful right now, in the depth of the deepest recession in forty years. When we resume world economic growth—particularly if the next boom is anything like the last one, with rapid inflation and bottlenecks developing in a number of industries—these other raw material cartels may become one of the most acute problems of the international economic order.[2]

---

[2] For a comprehensive analysis, see C. Fred Bergsten, "The New Era in World Commodity Markets," *Challenge*, September-October 1974, reprinted in *Toward A New International Economic Order: Selected Papers of C. Fred Bergsten, 1972-1974* (Lexington, Mass.: Heath-Lexington Books, 1975).

PART THREE

THE THREAT TO THE
INTERNATIONAL MONETARY ORDER

DISORDER IN THE INTERNATIONAL MONETARY SYSTEM

Takuji Shimano

Crisis and the Collapse of the System

We cannot right now predict how reform of the international monetary system will develop. Out of a series of conferences attended by the finance ministers and their deputies from twenty nations and meetings of the board of directors of the International Monetary Fund (IMF), the Morse Report was compiled and presented to the 1973 IMF General Assembly in Nairobi. At that time, the course of reform in the system seemed to have been determined. The outbreak of the fourth Middle East war in the fall of 1973, however, completely shattered the expectations of reform. The strategy of the oil-producing nations had a decisive effect on almost every country in the world, making the future of the international monetary system entirely uncertain. Deprived of a way to reform the system, we are now barely managing to keep international finance from bankruptcy through currency flotation.

Attempts at international monetary reform are further complicated by world-wide inflation. The current inflation is an inevitable consequence of the weaknesses inherent in the IMF system. Nixon's New Economic Policy was announced on August 15, 1971, suspending dollar-gold convertibility and imposing a 10 percent import surcharge. In effect the purpose of the new American policy was to offset the threat to the IMF system by shifting part of the burden to those nations that had surpluses in their international accounts. Compared with the past U.S. policy of benign neglect, and considering the international political context, the new policy was a clear indication that the United States was giving its national interests a vigorous push. From the perspective of the IMF system and its survival, how-ever, this step was unavoidable.

There are abundant studies and records of the collapse of the IMF system, and it may seem unnecessary to add one more view, but the recent oil crisis has made us poignantly aware that we live in a world where all nations are inter-dependent, and that this world is trapped in a dual crisis. It is vital that we try to grasp a more complete picture of the breakdown in the IMF system from the new perspective of the dual crisis. Robert A. Mundell, in his essay "The Crisis Problem," points out that collapse

75

is the breakdown of order, the subversion of an institutional parameter, and crisis is impending collapse. Collapse can come about either because certain boundary conditions are reached, or because the control mechanism is such that the equilibrium of the system is an unstable one.

Mundell calls the first cause of collapse a "structural crisis," and the second a "control crisis." To apply his formulation to our current concern, we may say the IMF system has already collapsed and the oil situation has reached crisis. I used the term "dual crisis" to indicate that the world economy is in an unstable state both in international exchange and in the allocation of natural resources. The two problems have both direct and indirect links that make it all the more difficult to reach any solution.

That the operation of international finance now hinges on currency flotation, albeit "managed" flotation, is clear evidence that the IMF system has indeed collapsed. It can no longer maintain the order that it was set up to provide. The collapse can be seen from the fact that flotation runs counter to the Articles of Agreement of the IMF, which have no provisions at all for flotation. In that sense, every country is now violating the IMF rules. Any discussion of international monetary reform will have to begin with the question whether a float should be permitted, a question that poses enormous technical and legal complications. Just what is a float? Of course, the general notion is that a float occurs when countries are not observing the parity margin. However, when the point is reached where even the basic lines of international monetary reform have yet to be established, it is absolutely impractical for the IMF to invoke even a provisional regulation authorizing its member countries to float their respective currencies.

One characteristic, and one weak point, of the IMF system was that its "boundary conditions" were asymmetrical between the United States and the other countries. Japan's foreign currency reserves, for example, are comprised of gold and dollars. But for the United States, the pivotal country in the system, the state of its gold reserves was the only boundary condition. Since boundary conditions are not symmetrical, it is apparent that the increase in the dollar supply of the United States (the U.S. deficit) would push world prices and income levels upward and world business conditions would improve. The reverse was also true. Hence, the controls of the system could function only in one of two ways. When countries other than the United States desired an increase in reserves, they could achieve that goal only through increased American deficits. If, on the other hand, they wished the U.S. dollar to maintain its value relative to gold, then those countries would have to lower their reserve levels—that is, create or exacerbate a deficit. This is known as the liquidity dilemma.

As the gap in the dilemma increases, it becomes harder to control the system and crisis occurs. The international monetary crisis during the latter half of the 1960s was a control crisis for the system. Adjustment in the exchange rates of the mark, franc, pound, and guilder by the major European countries was actually directed toward protection from world inflation caused by an oversupply of dollars. However, in the context of the international monetary system, readjustment of the exchange rate meant that the dollar-gold reserves of the Western European countries, the control variable in the system, could not any longer perform their control function. The IMF was able to maintain the fixed exchange rate only to the extent that the Western European countries could convert their dollar holdings into gold, thereby weakening the American gold reserve position and activating the control function that decreased the volume of money in circulation. The control crisis of the system reached the boundary conditions as the U.S. deficit in the balance of payments continued to increase, and the situation moved from structural crisis to collapse. For that reason, the announcement of Nixon's New Economic Policy signaled the total collapse of the IMF system.

The Problem of Gold: Gold—or What?—as an Exchange Standard

The January 17, 1975, international monetary conference in Washington, D. C., ended with a probe into possible forms of international cooperation on two problems: the recyling of surplus oil revenues accruing to the OPEC countries from the higher price of oil, and how to deal with gold. I would like to focus on gold, and ask whether it will be phased out of the monetary system altogether or whether it will be reinstated. The Group of Ten Washington conference seems to have been too preoccupied with immediate concerns to plan for the long-range future. Nevertheless, the ten countries agreed (1) that the official price of gold should be abolished on the assumption that the SDR was to be placed at the center of the international monetary system; (2) that investment in the IMF should be increased by 32.5 percent, for a total of approximately 39 billion SDRs; and (3) that IMF oil loan funds should be increased in 1975 by 5 billion SDRs.

The first of these, the proposed abolition of the official price of gold, merits special attention here. The rapid jump in gold prices on the London market to $187.50 an ounce on December 20, 1974, and the growing deficits in the international accounts of all countries since the oil crisis point to a definite need to revalue the price of gold. However, it must be remembered that the rising price of gold is not directly linked to international monetary reform. To put it succinctly, a higher price for gold does not necessarily lead to reinstatement of the precious metal in the international monetary system. France's revaluation of gold is proof that the central bank will not agree to sell its gold, much less give it up for control by an international agency like the IMF. A rapid rise in the free-market price of gold does not necessarily create incentives to use gold in international settlements. Can the world, then, afford to abolish the use of gold in the international monetary system?

It would certainly not be easy to do so. It would take some time before a substitute was found to replace gold as a reserve asset. When we discuss the soaring price of gold we are talking about gold as a commodity, not as a reserve asset. Excess liquidity based on excess dollars has led to global inflation, which in turn strengthens the urge to buy gold as a commodity. Gold then becomes no different from any other commodity whose price begins to soar.

Certainly the price of gold has steadily increased since the end of World War II. But abolition of the two-tiered price of gold on November 13, 1973, which followed the suspension of dollar convertibility, was decisive: it meant that the price of gold would be subject solely to free-market pressures. Consequently, the precipitous price rise in recent times is not the result of reserve-asset preference for gold, but is determined simply by market supply and demand. Thus, each country will sooner or later revalue its gold reserves at near-free-market rates. The United States has opposed revaluation until now. However, the market price is now four times the official price and even the United States does not have the ability on its own to release enough gold into the market to lower its price.

When a country revalues its gold reserves, the total reserves held by that country will automatically increase, as will the proportion of reserves held in gold. Considering these possibilities and the fact that the $2 billion loan West Germany recently extended to Italy was secured on gold, one is led to speculate that gold will eventually be reinstated in a central position. Any such speculation, however, would go wide of the mark. Gold has been used by all nations up till now as a reserve asset, but unless it takes on the additional function of a settlement currency, the convertibility of a given currency into gold will not be restored.

Second, in order to abolish gold as a currency, we must use something to replace it as a reserve asset. Under the gold exchange standard or gold/dollar standard system, the dollar was a perfect reserve asset as long as it was convertible into gold. However, under the gold/dollar standard system profit accrues to the dollar from the rest of the world in the form of seignorage. A future international monetary system must be a system that does not generate seignorage. More specifically, we need a new kind of reserve asset that will not require international settlements and reserves to be calculated by using a particular national currency (as, for example, the U.S. dollar). The only thing that qualifies as such a substitute at present is the SDR. Since SDRs can be managed internationally, the supply can easily be adjusted to the rate of expansion in the world economy. Thus, the supply will be free both from controls by an arbitrary policy of any particular country and from the disadvantage of gold, whose supply is physically limited. At present, however, the SDR is still inferior to gold as a reserve asset, since it does not have the confidence that gold has enjoyed by virtue of its long and secure tradition and its qualities as a precious metal.

78

Third, as I see it, there are two prerequisites for raising the level of confidence in the SDR and phasing out the use of gold in the international monetary system. One is the adjustment function in the balance of payments and the other is the method of settlement. The adjustment function is now performed by the "managed" float. Theoretically, a "clean" float would be more desirable than a "managed" float to cut down the role of foreign reserves, including the abolition of gold as a currency. Since that is not practicable, promoting the adjustment function will decrease the excessive interest in the level of international reserves. The introduction of an objective index should equalize the now uneven distribution between surplus and deficit countries. Such an index would provide a means for fast and narrow-range parity adjustments.

The second prerequisite is the introduction of the idea of assets settlement. As a method of settlement it is certainly practical, and the countries of the European Community have been using a similar method for some time. It is quite different from the previous practice of using a specific currency (such as the dollar) for international settlements. The assets settlement formula requires the debtor country to settle with the creditor in proportion to the percentages of its foreign reserves in gold, gold tranche, SDRs, dollars and other national currencies. If settlements are handled in this way, the component ratio of foreign reserves held by each country will tend to be equalized over a period of time. Consequently, the relative importance of specific reserve assets such as gold will also tend to converge toward roughly the same level for every country.

Assets settlements would be useful in limiting the volume of dollars and other national currencies used for reserves and in increasing the possibility that the SDR would acquire importance as a reserve asset. The SDR is not designed for private holdings, but only for settlements in international accounts. Because of its limited function, the central banks must from time to time intervene in the exchange market to help stabilize it. Hence there must be an intervention currency. If all countries were permitted to hold unlimited dollars for intervention purposes, the dollar would accumulate as the reserve currency insofar as it was stable. But then the international monetary system would remain as unstable as ever, and the whole purpose of instituting the SDR as a reserve currency would be defeated. Certainly, the dollar and other currencies will continue as intervention currencies for some time, but as reserve assets they should be limited to a necessary minimum to be used only for intervention purposes. The introduction of an objective index and assets settlement methods will be one of the required steps in establishing the limit.

The Problem of Gold: Gold and SDRs

The SDR will gradually become more important as a reserve asset and as a standard currency. At present, however, it is still too weak, in both credibility and volume, to take over for gold and the dollar. The next question is what role gold can play in the interim until the SDR becomes a viable alternative, but in fact whether gold will lose its position as a major reserve asset depends on how far the SDR can be developed as such a reserve asset. At the twenty-nation conference of finance ministers in June 1974, it was decided to index the SDR by the standard basket formula derived from the weighted average of sixteen national currencies. That means the SDR will be subject to the influence of inflation and gold revaluation in those countries. The SDR can still be made to function as a unit of calculation—that is, as a standard currency—so that the most challenging problem facing the future of the SDR is in fact its potential for replacing gold as a reserve asset. To place SDRs in the central position would mean that gold would be used for production purposes (higher social savings) and not as money, which would be almost universally agreeable as a positive step to ensure international economic welfare. On the other hand, if SDRs are not fully developed as a reserve asset, gold might very well be reinstated.

If only to guarantee the growth of the SDR, gold should perhaps be maintained as a reserve asset for the time being. Too hasty a reform that tries to abolish gold in one fell swoop would create further instability and run counter to the ultimate aim of replacing gold completely. The fate of gold—whether we put it back in its central place or get rid of it—comes down to the question whether we regard gold as a backup for an immature but potentially strong SDR or as a problematic factor in the effort to restore dollar convertibility. The latter approach would soon bring back the U.S. national currency as an international reserve. If we use gold for the sole purpose of strengthening the SDR, on the other hand, we would achieve the first international managed currency in monetary history.

An SDR-standard system has been envisioned as a way to create such a currency, but some believe that gold should be concentrated in the IMF alone, and the SDR be made convertible into gold to be fully functional both as a standard and as a reserve currency. This approach, however, would have to find effective solutions to certain problems in order to be at all viable.

First, if the SDR were substituted for the dollar rather than for gold, the international monetary system would develop into a three-layered structure built on gold, SDRs and national currencies including the dollar. By contrast, if the SDR replaced gold (not necessarily immediately), the structure would be double— SDRs and national currencies including the dollar. With the three-layer structure, the SDR would probably not be used as an intervention currency, making the SDR part of an international monetary system that was actually a gold/SDR standard system. Available gold is absolutely limited, and so as trade expands and economic growth accelerates, the number of SDRs issued would increase, posing the real danger that confidence in the SDR would wane—witness what

80

happened to the dollar when the supply began to increase far in excess of the official American gold reserve. To establish a working dual structure would require international consensus on the indexation of the SDR. This is admittedly a weak point, but since the SDR would not be pegged to gold, there would be no danger that confidence in it would decline because the price of gold rose. In the dual structure gold would be no more than a commodity.

Second is the question whether it would be possible to concentrate gold in the IMF. A revaluation of reserve assets by raising the official price of gold would increase the importance of gold as a reserve asset, and when that happened, most countries would find it impossible to subscribe their gold to the IMF. It would seem more realistic to help augment the international reserves of each country by increasing the SDR issue, thereby reducing the proportion of gold in the reserves. Effective concentration of gold under IMF management would be possible only if a reserve other than gold were fully developed and enjoyed universal confidence. Then it would be possible to establish a workable international monetary system centered on a substitute reserve asset, such as the SDR, rather than gold. By that time, for all practical purposes, gold would have ceased to function as currency.

The Floating Exchange Rate: Its Role in Adjustment

Simultaneously with the second devaluation of the dollar in February 1973, all major currencies were placed on a floating exchange rate. After two full years, the float has proven to be important in stabilizing (or at least preventing further instability in) international finance. If the previous fixed rates had remained in effect at the time of the oil crisis in the fall of 1973, that fact alone would have invited large-scale speculation, bringing the same kind of monetary crisis that had occurred several times since 1969.

The current inflation and its international repercussions, for which no effective cure has yet been discovered, seem to have diverted our attention from the stabilizing function of the float. The float has in fact contributed much to international stability during this crucial period for the world economy.

Clearly, however, fluctuations must be kept within certain limits in the fixed exchange rate system. In order to prevent the rate from rising it is necessary either to supply foreign currencies according to demand at the fixed rate or to buy all the national currency sold at that rate. Let us take the United States and Japan and ask how the two countries can maintain the present exchange rate. One choice is to supply dollars for which there is excess demand. To do that, Japan must use its foreign reserves or borrow from external sources. Another choice is to try to reduce the volume of dollars desired, to adjust the demand. The first approach pertains to the problem of liquidity, and the second to problems of adjustment. To achieve liquidity is to hold reserves (supply) adequate to meet demand, and to achieve adjustment is to attain equilibrium in demand and supply by adjusting demand. With liquidity, a solution should be possible through cooperation between the two countries concerned. The possibility that the liquidity level will reach what Mundell called "boundary conditions" seems minimal. For example, in order to prevent the exchange rate from topping 300 yen to the dollar, the United States has only to supply as many dollars as needed. To stop the rate from falling lower, all Japan has to do is to buy up any amount of dollars sold. Since Japan can print the amount of yen it needs, and the United States can do the same with dollars, it may seem that the problem of liquidity can be easily resolved.

We must note, however, that such a solution amounts to the two countries giving each other carte blanche on the security of their goods and services. The result of such credit transactions of goods and services would simply be an increase in the rate of inflation, and that could not long continue. From this it should be clear that the creation of liquidity alone will not solve the balance-of-payments problem between two countries, much less solve the entire international monetary issue. If liquidity is not to be created, the remaining choice is to keep using reserves or to borrow. However, there is a limit to the amount of reserves held, and continual deficits cannot be covered forever by using reserves. This is where the importance of adjustment lies.

The Floating Exchange Rate: Guidelines for the Float

We can see from our discussion that the problem is a simple one if the float is considered only in its adjustment function. Theoretically, the clean float is the fastest and best way to achieve equilibrium in the international balance of payments. Under a clean float it is not necessary to have enormous reserves on hand, and the components of the reserves, the way of handling gold, and the development of SDRs all become irrelevant.

In reality, however, there are many factors that do not permit the use of a clean float. According to the December 1974 *Economic Outlook* of the OECD, the factors contributing to instability in the world economy are (1) the uncertainty of the future of the economic outlook, (2) the lack of confidence in the ability of policy-making agencies to cope effectively with the serious and broad effects of the energy crisis, (3) doubts whether the market economy and the financial system can continue to function properly under the current spiraling inflation, (4) the effects on consumer behavior of the uncertainties generated by inflation and unemployment, and (5) the uncertainty about the structural adaptability of the economy during the energy crisis.

These factors contribute to the uncertainty surrounding the problem of balance of payments for every nation, but the situation is not one that calls for a return to the fixed rate. If more destabilizing factors pile upon one another, the danger arises that many nations will take arbitrary action on their own accord. It is precisely to prevent this from happening that the IMF and OECD are trying to encourage close international consultation and some monitoring of the process of adjustment.

The guidelines for the float come out of the same trend of thought. Those guidelines would not pave the way back to the fixed rate system: they would instead be a kind of emergency measure designed to check the danger that some countries will adopt a "beggar-my-neighbor" policy as they enter the competitive race to devalue their currencies to cope with stagflation. The conference of finance ministers of the Group of Twenty originally planned to set more explicit "Rules for Floating" rather than guidelines. It is, however, difficult to set limits on the float because the adjustment function of the float derives from the very fact that it fluctuates. Moreover, economic structures are qualitatively dissimilar from country to country and the problems the countries face also vary widely. Thus, it becomes extremely difficult to set rules for floating.

The guidelines have been formed around two different kinds of intervention: (1) "smoothing intervention" in daily fluctuations in the exchange rate, and (2) "moderating intervention" whose purpose is to narrow gaps in movements around the long-range trend by taking seasonal shifts in imports and exports into consideration. Following these guidelines, each nation is expected to adjust its exchange rate standard within a certain range. This is a form of international cooperation designed to get over the period of instability by making the best of the merits of the float. Consequently, these efforts are by nature emergency measures to reduce the present level of instability as far as possible, and as such they will not determine the course of international monetary reform. The implication is that for the near future no other method is as effective as the float.

THE THREAT FROM WORLD "INFESSION" AND THE OIL EXPLOSION

Robert Triffin

The first section of this paper tries to summarize, with record brevity, the long-run threats to the world economic, and particularly the world monetary, order. The second section illustrates what I regard as the major, and most intractable, of these threats by a critical review of prevailing policy responses to the energy crisis.

The World "Infession"

The threats that confront mankind, as we enter the last quarter of this century, pervade the financial, economic, social and political fabric of the entire world. I shall group them under four headings, but they may be summarized in a single word not to be found yet in any dictionary, "infession"— that is, an inflationary recession, or even depression, reflecting the bankruptcy of the traditional answers given to changing economic problems both by the free market mechanism and by the interventionist policies of national governments, at home as well as abroad.[1]

An Incipient World Depression? The signs of an incipient world recession—or even depression—are multiplying everywhere. The growth of real GNP, nearly uninterrupted since the end of World War II, has now slowed down significantly or even in a considerable number of countries has reversed. In the United States GNP actually declined by 5 percent from the last quarter of fiscal 1974 to the last quarter of fiscal 1975, and at an annual rate of 9.4 percent in the latter alone. For the Organization for Economic Cooperation and Development (OECD) as a whole, the rate of growth in GNP is estimated to have dropped from 6.3 percent in 1973 to one-fourth of 1 percent in 1974, and is projected to be one-half of 1 percent for 1975.

Unemployment has risen to well over three million in the countries of the European Community and is expected to have grown to three and a half or four million by spring 1975. In the United States, unemployment is already close to eight million and is expected to rise throughout all or most of the rest of 1975.

---

[1] The term "infession" was suggested to me by my son, Nicholas Triffin, as reflecting more accurately than "stagflation," "slumpflation," or "depflation" the temporal and causal sequence from inflation to recession or depression.

In the less developed countries unemployment or underemployment fears are dwarfed by the prospect of starvation this year for hundreds of thousands of people.

The human misery entailed in this makes it nearly indecent to mention the financial threats intertwined with it. Interest rates, both long-term and short-term, have soared to two or three times their previous levels over the last decade and yet failed to attract investors. The volume of Euro-bond issues, for instance, fell from $6.7 billion in 1972 to less than $1.5 billion in 1974. Borrowers and banks have been forced into an enormous expansion of shorter-term credits, now slowed down by widespread fears of bankruptcies, while monetary authorities continue to squabble about who should shoulder the task of "lender of last resort," especially in the so-called Euro-currencies—or, better, "xeno-currencies"—markets.

A Long-Entrenched World Inflation. This incipient world depression could hardly be blamed—as depression most often could in the past—on the deflationary errors of national governments or of the world monetary and financial system. It is, indeed, largely the result of excessively "permissive" or "accommodating" rates of expenditure levels far in excess of available production capacity. Consumer price increases are now averaging 14 to 15 percent a year for the OECD countries—with only two countries with smaller than two-digit increases: Germany (5.6) and Switzerland (7.6)—and the average is higher still in most less developed countries.

A large part of this monetary and credit expansion escapes "national sovereignty" controls. In the eight European countries reporting external liabilities and assets of banks in domestic and foreign currencies, the "controlled" domestic money supply rose by about two-thirds in the short space of four years (1970–1973), but Euro-currencies liabilities tripled, and the combined total nearly doubled. Domestic inflationary trends in the United States were slowed down by the absorption of excess dollars by foreign central banks—accelerating inflation abroad—to the tune of about $60 billion to $70 billion in these four years. Money supply, narrowly defined, rose by slightly less than 30 percent, but quasi-money by 90 percent and the combined total by 58 percent. I shall refrain from the temptation to say what such inflation rates would mean if extrapolated over another ten- or twenty-year period.

Unprecedented International Disequilibria. Until the explosion of oil prices in the fall of 1973, the U.S. deficits were by far the major factor in the world international payments disequilibria. Measured by U.S. net reserve losses—including rough estimates of Euro-dollar liabilities to foreign central banks—they totaled, over the four years from 1970 through 1973, more than $70 billion, of which more than 90 percent was financed by foreign central banks' dollar accumulation and by inflationary issues of high-powered reserve money.

The OPEC countries are now expected to accumulate current-account surpluses of about $60 billion in a single year. Published information on their accumulation of official monetary reserves in 1974 (about $32 billion) suggests that this accumulation will have financed about half their current surpluses, the other half having been financed by other forms of capital outflows, public and private.[2]

International payments disequilibria thus continue to be financed very largely—as they did in previous years—by inflationary rates of expansion of world monetary reserves: some 21 percent in 1974, as against an average annual increase of 24 percent in the previous four years. About 90 percent of this expansion continues to be fed by the accumulation of foreign exchange—primarily dollars and Euro-dollars—as reserves by the surplus countries. Relatively few countries (particularly Australia, Sweden, Israel, and Denmark) have experienced any substantial declines in gross reserves so far, the huge current-account deficits of Britain, Japan, Italy and France having been fully financed and even over-financed by capital imports. In December 1974 the global gross reserves of non-OPEC countries, both developed and developing, still exceeded by nearly $6 billion their bloated levels of December 1973.

The generalized recourse to floating exchange rates has not so far degenerated into beggar-my-neighbor devaluations, nor slowed down the strong expansion of international trade, but might yet do so in the future if the present incipient recession developed into a full-blown world depression. On the other hand, wild fluctuations in gold prices and foreign exchange rates obviously entail considerable costs and risks—including bankruptcies—for normal transactors as well as speculators. Even the most enthusiastic devotees of flexible rates can hardly claim that they have arrested previous inflationary trends in international reserves and domestic money creation, that they brought about a more satisfactory equilibrium in the world's balance-of-payments network than had been previously established, or that they can provide a constructive answer to the new disequilibria arising from the energy crisis.[3]

The Bankruptcy of Economic Management. The three broad threats summarized above obviously reflect a total failure of national governments to implement the often-repeated goals of their economic policy—that is, the "holy trinity" of

---

[2] Most encouraging in this respect is the sharp rise of OPEC financial assistance to the LDCs. Total aid commitments are estimated well above $20 billion already, and actual disbursements in 1974 at more than $4 billion—that is, about 3 percent of the reporting countries' combined GNP.

[3] The German mark rose by more than 70 percent against the dollar from 1968 to July 1973, declined by 17 percent in the next six months, and rose again by about 22 percent from January 1974 to February 1975. This enormous appreciation has not decreased German surpluses on goods and services, which rose, on the contrary, from $4.8 billion in 1968 to $10.1 billion in 1973 and at an annual rate of nearly $15 billion in the first three quarters of 1974.

continued economic growth, reasonably stable prices, and tenable balance-of-payments equilibrium. Inadequate policy responses to changing world problems may indeed prove to be the most obdurate "threat to the system," as the new problems confronting us are unlikely to be satisfactorily solved by either of the two ideologies which divide economists as well as politicians.

The laissez-faire free market mechanism is better able to promote an efficient use of available resources than to husband and allocate them wisely in scarcity situations. "Charging what the traffic will bear" becomes in such situations a spur to inflationary price and wage increases as well as an inhuman way to distribute the burden between the rich and the poor and between essential needs and profligate waste.

Interventionist policies, on the other hand, have been successful at fighting recessions, but have yet to learn how to fight inflation, especially when inflationary trends are not of the "demand-pull" variety. They have hardly faced yet the "infession" problem that now confronts us and defies the Keynesian prescription for either depression or inflation. Buridan's ass starved for being unable to choose: our economists and politicians are more likely, in the end, to choose the policies that they know best, and that are more popular with the voters—they will fight depression, but by methods that are likely to aggravate the inflation which is in fact one of the main causes of the emerging depression.

I do not pretend to have any satisfactory way of meeting these problems simultaneously. I am convinced, however, that the new policies for which we are groping will have to meet both of the following imperatives: first, that high rates of unemployment have an unacceptable, political and human cost, and cannot be tolerated for long by any democratic society, and second that, as long as price increases themselves also exceed tolerable levels, unemployment should not be combatted through traditional macroeconomic policies of deficit spending (tax cuts and increases in expenditures), financed by inflationary rates of monetary expansion, lest increased borrowings from the public trigger further increases in interest rates.

What is called for, instead, are selective policies channeling any increased spending in the directions in which it will do the most good, and extracting from these policies all that is possible to moderate "cost-push" price and wage increases. I would mention, as specific examples, labor retraining programs, public service jobs, and selective spending programs.

Labor retraining programs and public service jobs. These should be "on tap" far in excess of what is now contemplated by the administration and should be available to any who are unemployed. They would be far less costly than aggregative expansionist policies, many of which would refuel inflation before "trickling down" to reduce hard-core unemployment. Federal subsidies should encourage local authorities and even "do-good" private groups to develop programs to improve the environment and the quality of life. This could elicit, at minimum cost, enthusiastic support and participation by many people—especially the young—increasingly and rightly concerned with these issues.

Selective spending programs. The industries worst affected by recession— or, on the contrary, by shortages—should also be aided by selective policies directly promoting the kind of spending that best fits long-term needs: (1) the automobile industry, for instance, should not be encouraged to produce more gas-guzzling cars, but helped to retool itself for the production of low-gas-consumption cars and mass-transportation buses, railroad cars, and so on; (2) oil-depletion allowances and other tax reductions to business firms should be abolished and replaced by direct subsidies aimed specifically at the kinds of exploration and research and development they are designed to encourage, rather than available for any purpose whatever, including the acquisition or expansion of control over other related or unrelated firms. The obvious difficulty in defining and enforcing these selective policies is that they risk being administered in a way more responsive to influential lobbies—and political contributions, even in the blatant form of "loans" cancelled later by the lenders presumably upon value received—than to the public interest.

Rather than dwell upon this awesome challenge to democratic forms of government (and other forms), let me venture, instead, a few remarks on current policy responses to the oil price explosion, which I have purposely skirted so far. These policy responses illustrate the point I have just made about the inability of economists as well as of governments to implement their best (and intellectually agreed-upon) intentions and policy objectives. This inability is as evident for domestic policies as for international policies where the policy makers are still wrapped up in the mutually defeating illusions of increasingly powerless "national sovereignties."

Misdirected Policy Responses to the Oil Crisis [4]

Before criticizing them, let me first congratulate our political leaders for their major oratorical reaction to the oil crisis. They are vying with one another in proclaiming *"urbi et orbi"* that the only hope of averting catastrophe is an expansion of international cooperation without precedent in world history. They should also be congratulated on the pledges negotiated with a number of countries for eschewing "beggar-my-neighbor" policies, and on their efforts to put together various "recycling" plans that are undoubtedly as indispensable in the short- or even

---

[4] There is far more agreement today on the controversial arguments and doubtful forecasts ventured in this section than at the time (September 1974) a first draft of it was prepared for presentation and discussion at a round-table meeting of the International Center for Monetary and Banking Studies in Geneva.

medium-run as they will prove inadequate in the absence of tougher long-run answers to the present disequilibria in world payments.

The Shelving of International Monetary Reform. The first of these responses has been to "put on ice"—or postpone to the calends of Greece—the plans for international monetary reform previously regarded as essential after eleven years of interminable debates and the utter collapse of the international monetary order. The balance-of-payments disruptions and uncertainties flowing from the oil crisis make all governments even more reluctant than before to tie their hands today by international commitments that they might feel unable or unwilling to honor tomorrow. This is perfectly understandable, but nevertheless regrettable (to say the least) for two reasons—the balance-of-payments disruptions and the oil crisis.

The most formidable balance-of-payments disruptions and world inflation ever experienced in man's history preceded, and contributed to, the explosion of oil prices, and their seeds would still be with us tomorrow even if the oil problem itself could be solved. Their basic roots admittedly lie outside the monetary field. They lie in the growing shortages of crucial industrial and agricultural materials arising from 200 years of unprecedented increases in material production, increases that since World War II have no longer been interrupted and slowed down by cyclical recessions, increases further aggravated by the incredible increase in world military expenditures to well over $200 billion a year.[5] "Charging what the traffic will bear" has enabled more and more sectors of the economy to raise prices, profits, and wages at an accelerated pace.

This being said, it nevertheless remains clear that sectoral price and wage increases could not have been transmitted to the economy as a whole if they had not been financed and underwritten by "permissive" or "accommodating" rates of monetary expansion far exceeding what could be absorbed by actual increases in production. Again, the permissive role played by national monetary authorities in this process is easily understandable, since determined anti-inflationary restraints of the traditional variety might in many cases have spelled temporary recessions, bankruptcies, and unemployment unacceptable to political leaders and public opinion.

Until about 1968, however, inflation remained primarily a national phenomenon, sanctioned inevitably by balance-of-payments deficits, depletion of international reserves and eventual currency depreciation (measured in terms of the currencies of the least inflationary countries). Dollar prices of internationally traded goods rose by less than 1 percent a year, on the average, from 1963 to

---

[5] Economic as well as political considerations make it particularly difficult to finance military expenditures in noninflationary fashion. This is undoubtedly one of the explanations of the spectacular postwar switch from an intractable "dollar shortage" to an equally intractable "dollar glut" as the main burden of military expenditures switched from Europe and Japan to the United States.

1968. But these price increases accelerated abruptly in the following years to annual increases of about 5 percent from 1969 through 1971, 8 percent in 1972 and nearly 30 percent from the third quarter of 1972 to the third quarter of 1973—well before the explosion of petroleum prices in the last quarter of that year.

This shift from national inflations to worldwide inflation was made possible by the extension of monetary permissiveness from the national to the international monetary institutions and policies. The world supply of international monetary reserves grew only moderately from the end of 1949 to the end of 1969, by about $32 billion over twenty years—that is, less than 2.7 percent per year. In the next three years, however, it grew ten times faster, at an average rate of nearly 27 percent per year, increasing more in this brief span of time than in all previous

Table 1
GROSS INTERNATIONAL RESERVES: 1969–1974
(in billions of $U.S.)

	Year-end			
	1969	1972	1973	1974
Non-OPEC countries	74.0	148.1	169.6	175.4
Developed	62.6	126.8	139.3	141.2
LDCs	11.3	21.3	30.3	34.2
OPEC countries	4.2	10.9	14.5	46.6
Middle East	1.6	4.6	7.2	27.3
Saudi Arabia	0.6	2.5	3.9	14.3
Iran	0.3	1.0	1.2	8.4
Iraq	0.5	0.8	1.6	3.3
Kuwait	0.2	0.4	0.5	1.4
Other Africa & Asia	1.6	4.4	4.7	12.4
Nigeria	0.1	0.4	0.6	5.6
Libya	0.9	2.9	2.1	3.6
Algeria	0.4	0.5	1.1	1.7
Indonesia	0.1	0.6	0.8	1.5
Latin America	1.0	1.9	2.7	6.9
Venezuela	0.9	1.7	2.4	6.5
Ecuador	0.1	0.1	0.2	0.4
Total	78.1	159.0	184.1	222.0
Gold	39.1	38.8	43.1	43.7
SDRs	—	9.4	10.6	10.8
Reserve positions in IMF	6.7	6.9	7.4	10.8
National reserve currencies	32.3	103.9	122.9	156.6

Source: *International Financial Statistics,* April 1975.

years and centuries since Adam and Eve. This was essentially the result of the international monetary system called the "gold-exchange standard"—under which foreign countries in fact accepted a national currency (the U.S. dollar) in settlement of most of their balance-of-payments surpluses, financing and thereby perpetuating enormous U.S. deficits, and correspondingly increasing their own issues of central bank ("high-powered") money. These issues of central bank money were multiplied in turn by the commercial banks under the traditional system of fractional reserve requirements for their own deposit liabilities. The cumulative deficits of the United States over these three years came to nearly $62 billion, more than 90 percent of which were financed by the accumulation of dollar IOUs by foreign central banks.

The international monetary system had thus become a main engine of world inflation, until it collapsed into the generalized system of floating exchange rates under which we live today and which of course provides no effective barrier against inflation, either national or international. (World reserves, measured in dollars, grew indeed at an annual rate of 16 percent in 1973 and 21 percent in 1974, while export prices of industrial non-OPEC countries rose by 27 percent in 1973, and at an annual rate of 26 percent in the first three-quarters of 1974.) Such a collapse was perfectly predictable—and widely predicted—in the absence of two basic and inextricably intertwined monetary reforms on which intellectual agreement had finally been reached in the late 1960s. The basis of these reforms were: (1) the need to adjust liquidity creation to the noninflationary requirements of potential growth in world trade and production, rather than to the vagaries of the private gold market and the U.S. balance-of-payments deficits; and (2) the need for a symmetrical enforcement of balance-of-payments discipline upon all countries alike—that is, not only upon surplus countries as well as upon deficit countries, but also upon so-called "reserve center" countries as well as upon other countries.

I rejoice at the endorsement of this analysis by Dr. Emminger [6] but confess my surprise at seeing it presented as a rebuttal to the "Triffin school" fears of a "deflationary bias . . . belied by actual developments." [7] What I had repeatedly predicted in fact over the last fifteen years was that the gold-exchange standard was bound to lead either to worldwide deflationary pressures if the United States corrected the deficits that were feeding most of the legitimate and needed increases in world reserves, or, if our deficits continued, not to world deflation, but to an eventual *Gold and Dollar Crisis*—the very title of my book—reflecting the inability of the United States to honor the gold-convertibility commitment on which the system was anchored.

---

[6] Notably in his Per Jacobsson lecture of June 16, 1973, on "Inflation and the International Monetary System," published by the Per Jacobsson Foundation, International Monetary Fund.
[7] Ibid., pp. 7 and 35.

"Actual developments" did not "belie" what was correctly called by Mr. Altman [8] "the Triffin dilemma," but fully confirmed the second of the two alternative outcomes it predicted. The real culprits, it seems to me, were not the "Triffin school" advocates of the substitution of controlled SDR for uncontrolled dollar-reserve creation, but the central bankers who for many years resisted such a reform, preferring to gamble on a restoration of the dollar strength, and even today are still arguing that a proposal to which "everybody has subscribed"—that "the role of reserve currencies should be reduced"—is long and "difficult to implement . . . in practice." [9]

A second reason for keeping alive a suggestion about international monetary reform to which—again to use Dr. Emminger's words—"everybody has subscribed" is that it is particularly appropriate for dealing with the present oil crisis as well as with other problems still confronting us. If it had been implemented in time, it would have resolved in advance much of the so-called "recycling" problem which the proposed "Witteveen facility" has belatedly tried to resolve on an ad hoc basis and a quantitatively inadequate scale—now to be supplemented (outside the IMF framework) by the latest Kissinger-Simon proposal for a $25 billion recycling fund or "safety net." All countries would have been committed to accumulating most of their future surpluses in reserve accounts with the fund—to be recycled, or sterilized, according to internationally agreed criteria and objectives—rather than being left free to invest such surpluses as they wished and to trigger currency crises by switching them at any time from one national currency or Euro-currency into another, for political or speculative reasons.

The OPEC countries may admittedly be less willing today to negotiate such a commitment than they might have been when it would not have singled them out as the major countries expected to relinquish their "sovereign right" to invest their reserves as they pleased. Yet the agreement of other countries to such a commitment, with appropriate guarantees and earnings, might make it more acceptable to all, and might in fact reduce the huge exchange risks now inseparable from reserve accumulation, strengthening the ability of the international community to meet other yet unforeseen crises.

The main obstacle to a worldwide agreement of this sort in the immediate future remains the unwillingness of the United States to restore convertibility at stable, even though adjustable, rates and its preference for a greater freedom of exchange rate flexibility than most other countries are willing to accept. This unwillingness should, however, prompt the countries of the European Community to accelerate, rather than slow down, the initial stages of their ambitious plan for economic and monetary union. I tried to spell out in my recent inaugural lectures

---

[8] In his article on "Professor Triffin on International Liquidity and the Role of the Fund," *IMF Staff Papers,* May 1961.

[9] Emminger, "Inflation and the International Monetary System," pp. 28, 43.

for the new Paul-Henri Spaak Foundation [10] the arguments for relatively modest and negotiable measures aiming at the creation of a "European Exchange Area" designed to achieve the maximum degree of exchange rate stability and agreed readjustments feasible among participating countries and to facilitate consultations with other countries—particularly the United States—on the management of their exchange rate relations.

This is not the place and time to repeat these arguments and suggestions but I remain convinced that the acceleration of regional as well as worldwide negotiations on international monetary reforms would be a better response to the oil crisis than the apparent resignation to their unnegotiability advocated today by many official advisers and academic experts.

Recycling Finance and Real Transfers

While applauding the current efforts to provide adequate international machinery for the "recycling finance" that will undoubtedly be indispensable over the next few years, I believe that more emphasis should be placed on the means of encouraging the real transfers and balance-of-payments readjustments necessary in the long and even the medium run to make such financing acceptable to the debtors as well as to the creditors. The stupendous estimates of OPEC accumulation and global recycling needs advanced in some responsible quarters (more than $600 billion by 1980 and $1.2 trillion by 1985) are entirely unrealistic in this respect. They vastly underestimate the feasibility of real transfers and adjustments.

Exporting Capacity of the Oil-Importing Countries. Measured in GNP terms, the real transfers entailed by the increase in oil prices, even on the most pessimistic assumptions recently advanced, would be on the order of 1 to 2 percent a year for the OECD as a whole (with a maximum of 6 percent for Ireland and less than 4 percent for Italy [see Table 2]). Spread over two or three years, such shifts would amount to only a fraction of normal annual GNP increases and be comparable in size to shifts that many countries have repeatedly experienced in the past as a result of similar changes in their terms of trade.

The moral outrage sometimes expressed over the inequity of such transfers is certainly indefensible. In 1974, per capita levels of GNP in most of the "new rich" OPEC countries remained, even after the quadrupling or quintupling of oil prices, only a fraction of GNP per capita in the "new poor" countries of the industrialized world. For eight countries [11] accounting for well over half of OPEC

---

[10] Brussels, November 4-6, 1974, largely reproduced in the *Echo de la Bourse* of November 4-7, and an English translation which is published in the March 1975 issue of the *Banca Nazionale del Lavoro Quarterly Review*.

[11] Venezuela, Gabon, Iran, Iraq, Algeria, Ecuador, Nigeria and Indonesia.

oil earnings, they probably average no more than $550—that is, about one-eleventh of the U.S. level and one-seventh of the average level in the European Community. They range from highs of about $1,850 in Venezuela, $1,540 in Gabon, $940 in Iran and $930 in Iraq to as low as $100 in Indonesia, as against more than $6,000 in the United States and $4,000 in the European Community in 1973 (see Tables 2 and 3).

Absorptive Capacity of the Oil-Exporting Countries. The main significance of the figures just quoted is not limited to moral issues which economists are neither more nor less qualified to debate than the man in the street. The figures are highly relevant to an objective appraisal of the main obstacle to real transfers and readjustments—that is, the fact that the oil-importing countries cannot solve their problem by exporting more to each other, but will have to export more to oil-exporting countries whose absorptive capacity has been greatly underestimated in the current debate over the oil crisis.

A determined effort by the industrial countries, through their own know-how and through exports of equipment, to accelerate economic development and diversification in the oil-exporting countries should meet no insuperable obstacles in the majority of those oil-exporting countries. One cannot help being struck, in this respect, by the sharp contrast between the emphasis placed on "recycling finance" in economic and political discussions of the oil problem in the oil-importing countries and the opposite emphasis placed on development plans and imports in most responsible statements emanating from the OPEC countries. Planned 1974 expenditures announced and budgeted by the seven major OPEC countries absorb more than 60 percent of the most optimistic estimates of their oil earnings.

More than 55 percent of anticipated oil exports come from the eight countries mentioned above, whose absorptive capacity for investment and consumption imports undoubtedly exceeds their earnings, even at the new oil prices. There should be no problem in these so-called "new rich" nations spending—and indeed overspending—the full amount of their GNP earnings per capita, earnings which are still only a fraction (one-sixtieth to one-third) of those of United States residents.

Another third of anticipated oil earnings comes from two countries (Saudi Arabia and Libya) with GNP per capita of roughly $2,900 and $5,800, respectively, at the new oil prices. Again, the spending of income at these levels should raise no insuperable obstacles, although the process is likely to be somewhat slower. It could be accelerated by a determined effort of the oil-importing countries to seek recycling finance through advance payments on firm orders and commitments for investments designed to improve and diversify the economic infrastructure of the OPEC countries and help them find necessary substitutes for

Table 2

OECD COUNTRIES: 1973 GNP ESTIMATES AND
1974 CURRENT ACCOUNT IMBALANCES AND INCREASES IN NET OIL EXPENDITURES

	1973 Population (millions)	1973 GNP		1974 Current Account ($ billions)		Percent of GNP	
		Total ($ billions)	Per capita (U.S. dollars)	Total	Increase (−) in net oil expenditures from 1973	Current account	Increase in oil exports
European Community	256.18	1,057	4,125	−15.85	−25.60	−1.5	−2.4
France	52.13	257	4,930	−7.50	−6.25	−2.9	−2.4
Germany	61.97	348	5,620	9.00	−6.25	+2.6	−1.8
Italy	54.89	138	2,520	−8.30	−5.00	−6.0	−3.6
Netherlands	13.44	60	4,440	1.50	−0.50	+2.5	−0.8
Belgium-Luxembourg	9.76	(45) [b]	4,570	0.25	−1.25	+0.6	−2.8
United Kingdom	55.93	175	3,130	−9.00	−5.25	−5.1	−3.0
Ireland	3.03	6.7	2,210	−0.60	(−9.40)	−9.0	−6.0
Denmark	5.03	27	5,440	−1.20	(−0.70)	−4.4	−2.6
Other Western Europe	121.33	259	2,135	−8.95	(−6.15) [b]	−3.5	(−2.4) [b]
Switzerland	6.44	41	6,430				
Austria	7.52	28	3,710	−1.00		−3.6	
Spain	34.86	57	1,640	−3.00		−5.4	
Sweden	8.14	48	5,920	−0.70		−1.5	
Norway	3.96	19	4,735	−1.35		−7.1	
Finland	4.66	17	3,660	−1.10		−6.5	
Other [a]	55.75	(49)	(885) [b]	−1.80		−3.7	

Other OECD	356.97	1,896	5,310	−12.70	−27.25	−0.7	−2.9
United States	210.40	1,295	6,155	−3.25	−14.75	−0.3	−1.1
Canada	22.13	119	5,370	−1.50	+0.25	−1.3	+0.2
Japan	108.35	413	3,815	−4.75	−12.00	−1.2	−2.9
Australia	13.13	58	4,400	−2.40 }	−0.75	−4.1 }	−1.1
New Zealand	2.96	11	3,640	−0.80 }		−7.2 }	
Total OECD	734.48	3,212	4,373	−37.50	−59.00	−1.2	−1.8

a Greece, Turkey, Portugal and Iceland.

b Estimated.

Sources: Population and rough GNP estimates are calculated from lines 99z, 99a and ra of *International Financial Statistics*, December 1974. Estimates in columns 4 and 5 are from pp. 60, 61, and 63 of the OECD *Economic Outlook*, December 1974.

Table 3

OPEC COUNTRIES: ROUGH ESTIMATES OF 1974 GNP, OIL REVENUES, BUDGETED EXPENDITURES, IMPORT INCREASES, AND RESERVE ACCUMULATION

(in billions of U.S. dollars, except as otherwise noted)

	1973 Population (millions)	GNP Estimates		Oil Revenues	Budgeted Expenditure Plans	International Reserve Increases	Import Increases (percent)
		Total	Per capita (dollars)				
Low absorptive capacity							
Abu Dhabi	0.1	(5.00)	(50,000)	4.1	0.4	—	
Qatar	0.2	(2.00)	(10,000)	1.6	0.2	—	
Kuwait	1.0	8.50	8,500	7.0	1.9	0.9	
	1.3	15.50	11,920	12.7	2.5	0.9+	
Moderate absorptive capacity							
Libya	2.1	12.18	5,800	7.6	5.0	1.5	72
Saudi Arabia	7.8	22.62	2,900	20.0	6.0	(9.7)	64
	9.9	35.80	3,615	27.6	11.0	11.2	
High absorptive capacity							
Venezuela	11.2	20.72	1,850	10.6	4.0	4.4	
Gabon	0.5	0.77	1,540	0.4	(0.2)	—	144
Iran	31.2	29.33	940	17.4	10.1	7.1	80
Iraq	10.4	9.67	930	6.8	6.6	(1.8)	113

Algeria	15.4	8.16	530	3.7	5.0	0.5	33
Ecuador	6.5	2.73	420	0.8	0.5	0.1	76
Nigeria	59.4	13.66	230	7.0	4.9	5.0	47
Indonesia	124.0	12.40	100	3.0	4.5	0.7	53
	258.6	97.44	375	49.7	35.8	19.6+	
Total	269.8	148.74	550	90.0	49.3	31.7+	59

Sources: For population, GNP estimates and oil revenues: *IMF Survey*, February 3, 1975, p. 38. GNP estimates for Abu Dhabi and Qatar are further approximations based on oil revenues. For reserve accumulation and import increases: *International Financial Statistics*, February 1975, pp. 19 and 37. International reserve increases are extrapolated through December for Saudi Arabia and Iran, on the basis of January–November estimates. Import increases for the last twelve months reported are from the third quarter of 1973 to the third quarter of 1974, except for Iraq, Ecuador and Nigeria (second quarters) and for Saudi Arabia (first to third quarter). For budgeted expenditure plans: *Bulletin Financier*, Banque de Bruxelles, October 25, 1974, p. 2.

their depletable oil resources. Such advance payments should be far more desirable and acceptable to the lenders as well as to the borrowers than the alternative forms of financing still prevalent today—the highly volatile liquid claims or the long-term investments. Liquid claims expose the borrowers to sudden destabilizing switches from one currency to another, and expose the lenders to inflation risks and politically motivated "blocking"—especially in the event of a new war between Israel and the Arabs. Longer-term investments may be distasteful to the borrowers because of the foreign control they entail over domestic enterprises, and to the lenders because of fears of later expropriation and "re-nationalization." Advance payments on contracts for future deliveries should be more acceptable to all concerned and should promote the real adjustments indispensable in the long run.

This leaves out of account only a minor fraction (less than $13 billion, or one-seventh) of anticipated annual OPEC oil earnings at present prices, these coming from Kuwait, Qatar and a few Arab emirates with huge earnings and insignificant populations (estimated at about 1 million for Kuwait and less than half a million for Qatar and the United Arab Emirates together). This is the most spectacular evidence of the absurdity of the fact that outdated international political institutions ("national sovereignties") allocate such enormous and potentially disruptive control over essential world resources to a few hundred thousand people, or rather to a handful of oligarchic rulers. The rational solution of this problem is just as inevitable in the long run as it is unthinkable in the short. It clearly lies in the "internationalization" rather than the "nationalization" of such crucial world resources, as well as of many others. This is not to say, however, that the persistence of the present absurd arrangements is at all likely, even in the short run. In the interest of self-preservation, the rulers of these countries and emirates will be bound to respond to the enormous pressures placed on them to contribute a growing part of these resources to foreign assistance and development beyond their borders, and particularly to poorer lands in Asia and Africa—including especially other Arab countries, such as Egypt and Syria, with enormous "absorptive capacity" and low foreign earnings. Financial assistance commitments by these countries to the LDCs were estimated to come to well over $6 billion at the end of last year, and actual disbursements during the year over $1.2 billion, about 8 percent of GNP, or more than twenty times the proportion of GNP to foreign aid for the United States.

Let me mention in this respect the danger that industrialized nations may find it hard to resist the temptation to compete with one another in meeting the largest and most frightening part of the "absorptive capacity" of that part of the world—that is, an unquenchable thirst for sophisticated and costly weaponry. The powder keg that is now being filled and overfilled by Israeli, Arab and Iranian armament imports might make even more probable (as well as more horrendous) the eruption of an armed conflict that would as a minor by-product make totally irrelevant and meaningless all the hazardous forecasts upon which economic policies are now being shaped to meet the energy crisis.

In any case, the estimates of petro-dollar accumulation by OPEC have come down sharply in the recent past, so far confirming the "guesstimates" above. One January 1975 forecast [12] is that the accumulation of foreign assets by OPEC will reach a peak of $248 billion in 1978, and decline at an accelerated rate afterwards to $179 billion in 1980 (as against the $624 billion estimate of the World Bank, on page 21 of McNamara's *Address to the Board of Governors* at the September 1974 annual meeting). Further downward corrections in real terms might result from a possible weakening of oil prices in relation to other prices, and the consequent worsening of the OPEC countries' terms of trade.

Conservation against Development

My final plea to our policy makers and policy advisers would be to switch their order of priority from the development of new sources of energy to a better husbanding and more efficient use of available supplies.

We cannot, of course, make overnight changes in long-entrenched consumption habits and productive infrastructures derived from energy costs a quarter or a fifth of what they are today. But neither can we hope to develop overnight the new sources of equally costly—or even costlier—energy that are now being contemplated. The efficient allocation of resources should obviously call for a drastic shift of ultimate spending patterns by consumers as well as a shift of intermediate production patterns by industry, to reduce the total use of energy in the future at least in the industrialized nations.

The present overemphasis on new energy sources would add further fuel to the inflationary problem for two reasons. First, the enormous expenditures required to develop and exploit some of these new sources of energy would add to the income stream of consumers without being matched, for a long time to come, by corresponding increases in the goods and services available to them. Second, producers would have to be given indefinite guarantees of the higher prices needed to elicit such development and production, even if lower-cost supplies became available again in the future.

Alternative policies of energy conservation could on the other hand be anti-inflationary in the short run, particularly if they were based in part on tax increases (it is roughly estimated that each one cent tax increase on gasoline in the United States would produce about $1 billion in tax collections), could tend to reduce rather than increase present market levels of oil prices, could improve transporta-

---

[12] Forecast in *World Financial Markets* (Morgan Guaranty Trust), January 21, 1975, pp. 1-11, and particularly the table on p. 8.

tion efficiency through a shift from private to collective means of transport whenever possible, could correspondingly decrease the inconvenience of traffic congestion, parking problems, and air pollution that make private cars less attractive today, even to their users, than increasingly unavailable alternative and efficient public transportation, and could take account of the fact that the present international pattern of energy consumption cannot be maintained indefinitely in the future (as the rest of the world develops—as we all proclaim it should—some 7 percent of the world population cannot go on consuming one third of the world's energy, as is the case today).

Summary and Conclusions

We can trust the determination—if not necessarily the success—of economists as well as politicians in combatting the recession which is spreading misery around us. We cannot be as confident, however, of their ability to do so without refueling the world inflation from which this recession emerged yesterday and which might lead to a worse recession tomorrow, and even to a collapse of the world economic order.

Some of the initial policy responses to the oil crisis are particularly disquieting in this respect: the emphasis on developing new and costly sources of energy rather than on ways of reducing wasteful and polluting consumption of available supplies, the emphasis on recycling finance rather than adjustment, and, most of all, the indefinite postponement of basic international reforms and the continued financing of overall disequilibria through the widely inflationary rates of world reserve creation characteristic of the last five years.

COMMENTARY

Gottfried Haberler

It is a great pleasure to comment on the two stimulating papers by Professors Shimano and Triffin, which complement each other very nicely. Professor Shimano's paper goes into the technical details of monetary reform while Professor Triffin provides the broad sweep. For brevity's sake I shall not say much on the large parts of the two papers where I find myself in full agreement with the authors, but rather concentrate on some points where I disagree or where I place the emphasis differently. Let me mention, however, my agreement with Professor Triffin that the impact of the oil price rise on the industrial countries has been greatly—even hysterically—exaggerated. In the words of Hollis Chenery in an excellent article [1] (which served to correct earlier excessively alarmist statements by Robert McNamara, president of the World Bank), "the major consequences of the change in OPEC price policy stem more from its suddenness than from its magnitude." If it had come more slowly, spread over several years, the oil price "increase would have had little effect on world growth."

I fully agree with Professor Triffin that the inflationary explosion had started well before the oil crisis and that "inflation is, in fact, one of the main causes of the emerging depression." Here I may mention a minor verbal disagreement: "infession" seems to me a poor substitute for stagflation. If you do not like the word "stagflation" why not simply say "inflationary recession or depression" which is self-explanatory? Let me elaborate on Professor Triffin's statement that inflation is the main cause of this recession: inflationary recession or stagflation is simply a predictable later stage of inflation. If inflation continues for a long time—like the present inflation which has been going on with minor interruption since 1938— inevitably a stage is reached where an attempt to slow down (not stop or reverse) the inflation, or perhaps merely to slow down the rate of its acceleration, causes unemployment and slack: that is the essence of stagflation.

The main areas of difference between Professor Triffin and myself, and I believe also between Professor Shimano and myself (although I am not entirely sure because Professor Shimano is cautious on these issues), are these, and they are differences more in the distribution of emphasis than in substance: I have much more faith in the effectiveness of market forces to deal with scarcities and maintain

---

[1] *Foreign Affairs,* January 1975, p. 244.

equilibrium than Professor Triffin has and, I believe, than Professor Shimano has. This leads to a different evaluation of floating exchange rates. Shimano and Triffin seem to regard floating as a necessary evil which we have to accept for the time being until inflation rates come down and the oil price rise has been digested. Then we go back to "stable and adjustable rates." Because they want to go back to stable and adjustable rates, they want to rely much more than I do on international institutions such as the IMF to supervise, coordinate, regulate, direct, organize, control, and harmonize national policies and international trade and payments. Furthermore, they stress the problem of liquidity and international reserves much more than I do. For me the adjustment problem is much more important than the liquidity problem. Professor Triffin even wants "internationalization of crucial world resources" such as oil. He could not well avoid entrusting the United Nations with that task. In view of the recent behavior of that organization it makes me shudder to think what would happen if it were given real power. We suffer enough from an irresponsible U.S. Congress. Should we put on top of that an infinitely more irresponsible international congress?

But let me go back to economics. Triffin says "inflationary recession . . . reflects bankruptcy of the traditional answers given . . . both by the free market mechanism and by the interventionist policies of national governments." He later scores the "excessively 'permissive' . . . rates of expenditure levels"—permissive monetary and expansionary fiscal policies.

I strongly object to mentioning the "free market mechanism" as a culprit along with inflationary government policies as a cause of inflation and stagflation. On the contrary, I believe it can be shown that if we really had free competitive markets, including moderate competition in the labor market, stagflation would be impossible, at least on the present scale. Inflation, yes—stagflation, no. In the past, when markets—especially labor markets—were free or freer than they are now, there was a lot of inflation, but no stagflation on a dangerous scale. Stagflation requires wage-push by unions. Even downward rigidity of money wages would not be enough to explain stagflation. Downward rigidity of real wages can explain it, if you start from a wage level that is too high for full employment. Indexation of an excessive wage level would bring that about. But under moderately competive labor markets wages would not rise under high unemployment as they do now and the dilemma created by stagflation would be absent. Professor Triffin says that "the free market does a better job to promote an efficient use of available resources than to husband and allocate them wisely in a scarcity situation." I cannot accept that. I thought it was precisely scarcity situations with which all economics is dealing. The trouble with the oil problem is not that it is a "scarcity situation," but that it is monopoly. I agree that excessive "monetary and credit expansion" on the national and international level is at the root of the worldwide inflation. But I believe that Triffin overemphasizes the role of uncontrolled Euro-dollar markets or "xeno-currency markets" as he calls them. U.S. monetary policies have not been frustrated by the Euro-dollar market. The existence of the Euro-dollar market has frustrated American capital export controls, but it would not have prevented American policy makers from stopping inflation, if they really had wanted to. (By the way, I agree with Triffin that "sectoral price increases" cannot lead to general inflation except with the help of "permissive" monetary policy.)

Triffin is, of course, right that the American inflation, which started again in 1965 as a consequence of the decision to finance the war in Vietnam and, equally important, of the decision to finance rising expenditures at home by credit expansion rather than by higher taxes, spread abroad because the world was effectively on the dollar standard. But he cannot bring himself to state clearly that fixed exchange rates were a necessary condition for that spreading abroad. Under fixed rates and convertibility a U.S. inflation—as well as a deflation—must spread. Only floating can prevent the spread of inflation and deflation.

Triffin does, of course, not put forward the theory which is popular in certain circles that the inflationary explosion of 1973–1974 was the consequence of floating. (Obviously the opposite is true—rapid inflation made floating unavoidable, because there can be no agreement on a common inflation rate of 10 to 20 percent.) But he says, "the generalized system of floating . . . under which we live today . . . of course is no effective barrier against inflation." It is, of course, only a necessary, not a sufficient condition for any country to stay out of worldwide inflation. How could West Germany, Switzerland, and the Netherlands have inflation rates less than half that of some of their neighbors, Great Britain and Italy, if they did not let their currencies float up?

Triffin says floating did not prevent a further inflationary expansion of world monetary reserves of "about 19 percent in 1974." But his figures in his Table 1 do not support this statement. True, total reserves rose from $184 billion to $222 billion from 1973 to 1974. But the great bulk of this increase was in OPEC reserves. The reserves of non-OPEC countries remained practically unchanged.

I submit that OPEC balances are an anti-inflationary and not an inflationary factor. (I hope Triffin will agree with that. In fact, if my memory serves me, he recently made that point himself, although he forgets it when he inveighs against floating.) Obviously, it would be an inflationary move if the OPEC countries started to spend all the dollars they have amassed on additional imports. Triffin is right, by the way, when he says that they will spend their dollars sooner than most forecasters thought and that therefore the dreaded enormous accumulation of OPEC dollars will not occur. Most of those who were alarmed by the expected enormous accumulation did not realize that prompt spending of the oil money on imports would put inflationary pressure and a heavy immediate real burden on the oil-importing countries.

But why should OPEC dollars be different from non-OPEC dollars? The answer is simple. Non-OPEC dollars in the hands of foreign central banks were bought with national currencies. The Swiss National Bank and the German Bundesbank pay francs and marks for the dollars they buy. The Saudi Arabian National Bank (or whatever it is called) does not issue rials against the dollar. Needless to add, non-OPEC countries may react similarly to OPEC countries—for example by sterilizing the dollar balance—and some OPEC countries may react like non-OPEC countries—especially Venezuela and other oil producers with a broader economic base than Kuwait and Saudi Arabia.

Triffin admits that floating "has not so far degenerated into beggar-my-neighbor devaluations nor has it slowed down the strong growth of world trade." But he warns it might yet do so in the future. I would say this. The recession is slowing down world trade, and that is inevitable. But floating is just as important in recessions to ward off deflationary effects from abroad as it is in inflationary periods to ward off imported inflation. However, floating can protect only against generalized inflationary or deflationary monetary effects from abroad. It cannot protect a country from the real changes which are always associated with inflation and depression and their impact on particular industries—for example, from enormous changes in the terms of trade (including the oil price rise). Furthermore, recession breeds protectionist reactions. Protectionist policies are real changes from which floating cannot shield a country. But floating makes it easier to resist the temptation to use import restrictions to "protect" the balance of payments because contrary to what was the case in the 1930s, a country with a floating rate need not fear loss of reserves.

Competitive depreciation in the 1930s was the consequence of excessively rigid exchange rates which were adjusted only *in extremis,* and not the consequence of floating, as it is often said. There was very little floating in the 1930s. The American dollar was pushed down by government intervention in the market: this was competitive depreciation. The policy could achieve its purpose of stimulating the American economy (at the expense of others) only because the gold bloc countries held on to their gold parities.

Professor Triffin says "the main obstacle to a worldwide agreement of this sort," an agreement recommended by him to restore stable but adjustable exchange rates, is "the unwillingness of the United States to restore convertibility at stable, even though adjustable, rates and its preference for a greater freedom of exchange rate flexibility than most other countries are willing to accept." I confess I cannot see any indication of the preference of the other countries for a return to fixed rates.

What counts, of course, is revealed preference, revealed by policy actions, not lofty speeches at international gatherings and other ceremonial occasions. Even the French, who enjoy rhetoric on fixed exchanges, balance-of-payments disciplines for the United States, and gold—even the French let the franc float when it suited them. The Germans say openly that they need floating to keep their inflation rate down. The president of the Swiss National Bank, Dr. Leutwiler, said in a recent speech that floating is not an ideal system, but that it is indispensable to keep down the rate of inflation. René Larre, managing director of the Bank for International Settlements, said essentially the same. But my star witness is the staunchest advocate of fixed rates among American economists—our good friend Professor Charles Kindleberger. In a recent paper [2] (not yet published), after explaining at great length why fixed rates are good and floating is bad, he admits that floating in the last few years has worked fairly well. Then he sums up: "I nonetheless insist that a system of permanently fixed rates, adjusted only when policies go wrong and not from time to time as a regular device, plus the adoption of monetary and fiscal policies to make them work, are a first-best solution, attainable perhaps only in the very long run, but superior for world economic unity and coherence to floating rates, the movable peg, crawling peg and the like."

I fully agree that permanently fixed parities would be the ideal monetary system for the world—provided they can be established without imposing undue inflation or unemployment on any country and provided no country is forced to impose controls on the movement of goods and capital to keep its parity nominally fixed. A unified world currency would be still better, assuming it could be managed without imposing inflation or deflation on anybody. But, alas, we do not live in that kind of a world.

Professor Triffin implores the Europeans to go ahead, harmonize their policies and stabilize exchange rates among themselves: they should not wait, he says, until the Americans are ready to join. I only can say I wish him luck. But if I look at the European scene, at the differences in the inflation rate, I am afraid it will take a long time. In the meantime the world economy and world trade have to go on. I can see no other solution than to go on floating, probably in a more or less managed and "dirty" way.

One last comment that deals with a point Professor Shimano has made. I think we should distinguish between managed floating and "dirty" floating. Perhaps it is merely a difference in degree, but it is, I believe, an important distinction. I would speak of "managed" floating if the authorities merely intervene in the market by buying and selling in order to smooth short-run fluctuations or even to moderate the trend. "Dirty" floating means interventions in the market that go beyond buying and selling foreign exchange—dual markets, split exchange rates

---

[2] "Lessons of Floating Exchange Rates," paper presented at Carnegie-Mellon/University of Rochester Conference, Pittsburgh, November 15, 1974 (mimeographed).

for capital and current transactions (as the French had for a while), allocation of foreign exchange, and penalty rates for imports of certain commodities in the form of "import deposits" (as was recently practiced by Italy in violation of GATT, IMF, and EEC rules). The IMF should see to it that managed floating does not become dirty. The guidelines for floating which the IMF executive board has formulated go some way to outlaw dirty floating, but they do not go far enough.

William Fellner

I will try to follow some good examples here. Nobody was keeping to a written text, as I see, nor will I, but I will try to comment on a few topics that, I suppose, lend themselves to a general discussion.

Both these papers on which we are commenting are interesting. I will point to some problems where I would differ from the other views here expressed, so that perhaps a broader range of views can be presented. Let me begin with the statement that I am somewhat more optimistic about the guidelines for floating than Professor Shimano seems to be, although only the future can show if my degree of optimism is not over-optimism.

I would not be sure that these guidelines should be viewed as describing an emergency situation, emergency measures, or that the whole present period should be considered strictly transitory. A superior alternative, one which I certainly would not exclude, is that this is a period in which certain conventions and a tradition will start developing on how we should behave under conditions of managed floating. I do not think that one should give up hope on that. The central bankers are capable of developing certain modes of behavior that can serve as guidance for how to behave subsequently. I am not at all sure that what must develop from this is chaos.

On a more general level of social theorizing we can say that some countries have written constitutions, others have unwritten ones. We may also say that most of our actions in our lives are guided by conventions and by how we have been conditioned, rather than by written law. I think it quite possible that we will develop reasonable conventions, a reasonable tradition, as to how we are to behave in this kind of a currency system. As a matter of fact, I have not seen anything particularly unreasonable happening during the recent period. It may be a period of learning how to behave in these circumstances.

Let me say here just a few words about the role of the increase in dollar reserves in bringing about the present world inflation. I am not of the opinion that one has gotten to the root of this process by suggesting that we have had these large U.S. deficits, and these deficits were financed by the rest of the world, so that this gave rise to an inflation that everybody abhorred. I think it is more convincing to say that it was obvious that, given the Bretton Woods system, inflation was spreading and that the rest of the world did not prevent this from happening and was in fact trying to hold on to fixed rates—the obvious and clearly predictable by-product of which was a generalized inflationary process.

If I look at the modes of behavior of governments in general here and abroad, I am strongly impressed by the fact that the political decision-making process makes it very difficult to resist generating economic processes that bring short-run political advantages, even though the price that needs to be paid for these advantages subsequently is very high indeed. Inflationary processes are precisely of this kind. They are of this kind mainly because an inflationary process, when it gets going, is largely unanticipated and people consequently behave as if they were earning higher real incomes than they actually will turn out to have earned. This provides substantial economic stimulus for a while. Governments every-where—and that includes the government of the United States as well as the governments of a great many other countries—simply were not capable of resisting this temptation and they made use of all excuses that were available for engaging in inflation. I think this is at the bottom, at the root, of this process.

This expresses itself, technically, in the fact that the fixed rate system, or adjustable rate system, was not abandoned until a very late stage. And I may point out that much the greater part of the dollar reserves held in the countries abroad was accumulated in a period in which it was quite obvious that the dollar was not convertible into gold on any major scale. Furthermore, a significant part was accumulated during a period in which the dollar was even officially incon-vertible into gold. I would turn the causal sequence around. I would say that what was happening is that governments abroad found it no easier than government here to resist the temptation to provide stimulus to their own economies by inflationary methods, and these methods included adhering to an exchange rate system that led to large dollar inflows with inflationary consequences. The infla-tionary methods did provide a stimulus, for the most part because the public's expectations lagged behind the actual rate of inflation.

The international reserves which were accumulated in the most recent year—I agree with Professor Haberler—do not fall in the same category as reserves earlier acquired. There was no formal commitment whatever to accumulate these reserves; and practically the entire increase in 1974 was attributable to the accumulation of assets by the oil-exporting countries. This was their way of investing part of their trade surplus. One may, of course, say that the fact that the oil-exporting countries were accumulating these reserves in the forms in which they were does have to do with the way in which the international monetary system is set up, and I think Professor Triffin would say that this would not have happened if we had a system that required the accumulation of such assets in the form of IMF reserves.

This is indeed true. What I would try to add to this, however, is that the problem of these funds is one that could not be handled by the method of transferring decision-making power to international agencies in an unqualified way. The reason for this is, I think, the following: One very unpleasant and unpalatable aspect of the oil situation is that the oil imports are distributed by country differently from the OPEC's willingness to lend to various countries. That is to say, some countries are in a more difficult balance-of-payments situation than others, because the money does not flow back into those countries.

By the way, I think that something similar could develop, also, if the oil-exporting countries increased their imports steeply. Then also I would expect that the various customers of those countries would not benefit from the additional exports in the proportions in which they would have to benefit from them in order to overcome their balance-of-payments difficulties without painful adjustment. And behind this there is the fact that everyone who looks around in the world knows that the countries hardest hit will be helped out, to some extent, by other countries. Now, while it is quite reasonable to assume that they will indeed be helped out to some extent by other countries, I think it would not be reasonable to assume that other countries would accept an unqualified and unlimited commitment in this regard. No country will accept that kind of an unqualified commitment for an indefinite future. What really is happening, I think, is that the relatively well-to-do countries say, We will alleviate the adjustment problem for you by methods that are essentially methods of subsidization, provided you are cooperative—and we will see how this relationship develops. And the receiving countries say, We will be cooperative provided the others are sufficiently helpful—and we too will see how that kind of relationships develops.

This is a risky situation—one which nobody would dream up as an ideal or as an objective. But it has developed and I think that in these circumstances it is difficult to imagine that the entire problem should be transferred in advance to an agency that then would act according to firmly formulated criteria of investing those funds here or there.

Let me say just a last word about a problem on which Professor Haberler has also commented. This is the inflationary or noninflationary character of petro-dollar accumulations. I think Professor Triffin has in mind here the unregulated character of the Euro-dollar market. That is to say, that if you have an amount of dollars that the oil-importing countries are transferring to the oil-exporting countries, and these countries then accumulate a large part of this amount in the form of Euro-dollars, what is growing there is a market that is not subject to the same kind of discipline as a national market in which reserve requirements exist.

That, of course, is true. The Euro-dollar market does have those characteristics. But we must couple this problem, I think, with the question, where these dollars come from. That is, what sort of expenditures are suppressed when these dollars are transferred to the oil-exporting countries? And how do Euro-dollar accumulations affect the spending habits of those accumulating these assets? Finally, to what extent do national monetary authorities compensate for the effects?

That is, I think, really quite a subtle problem, because I think the best way of describing the nature of a Euro-dollar is to say that it is not itself a means of payment. You do not pay for goods and services in Euro-dollars. But Euro-dollars do in some sense enter into what one might call the Cambridge k-ratios in a somewhat extended sense, because they are very liquid assets and they are denominated in dollars. Each individual owner believes he can transform these into dollars in the United States any time; and each individual owner can indeed transform them any time into means of payments unless his bank fails. So Euro-dollars do affect liquidity ratios. Now, to what extent this influences the rate of spending of conventionally defined money in any one country is, I think, very speculative. I have not seen any convincing data on this.

Euro-dollars do increase liquidity, even if not with the same effectiveness as national currency holdings. But the whole question becomes complicated by a second aspect: the creation of Euro-dollars is associated with the transfer of dollars in a U.S. bank from specific owners to others who need not have the same spending habits. Further, we do not know to what extent the net change in liquidity and in spending habits influences the monetary authorities of the various countries in their own policies. After all, one would expect monetary authorities to react to observed trends in the rate of spending of conventionally defined money, and these are the trends about which we are talking when we consider the liquidity effect of Euro-currency holdings.

Let me finish by repeating that I thought that both these papers were exceedingly interesting, and that we have here a number of topics that are well worth thinking about and discussing.

J. Marcus Fleming

Like the other discussants, I find a great deal to applaud in the papers that were prepared for us by the principal speakers. However, the job of a discussant is to discuss—that is to say to disagree as far as possible, and I will do my best to disagree with what they have said, and, indeed, with what the other discussants have said.

My main reservations on Professor Triffin's paper might be summed up as follows: I think he imputes too much of the deflation to the preceding inflation, too much of the inflation to monetary expansion, too much of the monetary expansion to reserve expansion, and too much of the reserve expansion to the failure of countries to adopt the principles of international monetary reform. I might add, perhaps, that too much of that failure is imputed to the United States, but I will not go into that question.

The present deflation is no doubt due to the preceding and concurrent price inflation, insofar as the latter automatically increased or increases the tax bite in countries with progressive taxation, and insofar as the excesses of speculative inventory accumulation tend to evoke a reaction. But the main influence of inflation, in my opinion, has been indirect. Anxiety to check the price inflation, and unwillingness or inability to use the methods of wage and price control, have led governments to gear their demand management too much towards influencing prices, and too little towards influencing quantities, until it was too late.

Since governments must be regarded as responsible for their actions, I should say that this is in large part a self-inflicted recession—though, of course, the oil price increase also had a great deal to do with it. And in that connection, I must say that if one wants to use the new cussword "infession," then this oil price increase certainly deserves the use of that expression. It is the most "infessionary" act that could possibly have been committed, since it simultaneously stimulated price inflation and a demand deflation, or quantity deflation.

Now, on the relationship between inflation and money expansion, I have to admit that the acceleration of world inflation, from 1972 onwards, was preceded by an acceleration in the growth of the world money supply and in liquid claims on the xeno-currency market—like Professor Triffin, I am fond of that new expression—from 1970 to 1972. However, there was also a considerable budgetary and fiscal relaxation in the same years, as a reaction to the slowdown in economic activity in each preceding year from 1969 through 1971. I think there is some danger in emphasizing money alone as a crucial factor.

Finally, I think that in 1973–1974 and 1975, great importance must be attached to cost-push factors, noncompetitive pricing practices in goods and labor markets. The outstanding example of this, of course, is the oil price hike itself, but the effect of this was multiplied by the actions of others, in what Professor Triffin calls "charging what the market will bear." Incidentally, in his paper, I found a little difficulty in following him just at this point, because I was not quite sure whether he was condemning the whole principle of the market system and the profit system or whether he was confining his objections to monopolistic situations.

Some of this cost-push may have been defensive, in the sense that the labor groups, or other groups, were attempting to maintain their real incomes and were shedding whatever money illusions they may once have had. Whatever its causes, as a result of this cost-push and of the slowing down of monetary expansion, the velocity of circulation, of course, increased in 1973 and very markedly in 1974.

On the relationship between money and reserves, if you look back to the 1960s, you will find that the world's money stock showed some tendency to vary—as Professor Triffin implies—more or less proportionately with world reserves, though the trend-rate of the growth of money was considerably higher than the trend-rate of the growth of reserves. In the 1970s, however, while the supply of money, particularly outside the United States, varied in sympathy with the supply of reserves, it did not vary in anything like proportion to reserves. The surplus countries seem to have been unable to offset the entire primary effect of the reserve influx on the money supply, but they were generally able to prevent a multiplied expansion of money. If there had been better coordination between central banks and governments, better offsetting might perhaps have been possible.

The great expansion of reserves in 1974, as has already been pointed out by Professors Haberler and Fellner, did not correspondingly expand the supply of money, because the increase accrued very largely to the governments of oil-producing countries which have been able to sterilize a large part of it. Now Professor Triffin condemns countries for failing to accept the principles of mone-tary reform, particularly the principle of asset settlement—the principle that bal-ance-of-payments surpluses and deficits should be settled by the transfer of primary reserve assets and not through the accumulation by surplus countries of currency claims on the deficit countries.

I would agree with him that without the adoption of this principle, as a general rule, it is difficult and perhaps impossible to maintain any kind of inter-national control over the volume and growth of international reserves. However, I believe that he accepts this principle in too radical a way. There is a need for somewhat greater flexibility in reserve creation than could be attained under the system of SDR allocation alone. One can see that the need for reserves varies over time—that there is a variable need for international credit which will only be available, in practice, if the creditor countries acquire a reserve asset in exchange.

Triffin himself has always advocated reserve creation by a world central bank, or its equivalent, in which reserve creation would come into existence as the counterpart to the extension of credit or of discretionary investment by the central authority. The reform proposals also suggest that flexibility, in a sense, might be brought into the reserve system by the use of internationally supervised credit arrangements, or even (within limits) by the accumulation of currency claims. But all of these arrangements necessarily involve derogations from the principle of asset settlement.

I would go even further. I have some doubts whether any system of asset settlement, even if supplemented by internationally supervised credit arrange-ments, could have coped with the balance-of-payments situation arising out of the oil price increase as efficiently as has the anarchical system of reserve creation through the xeno-currency market which Triffin has described. A pure asset settlement system, obviously, would have been extremely deflationary in its effects, but with all my desire as an international official to support the idea of international control over the provision of credit and reserves, I cannot help feeling that in this particular crisis anything that could have been done by international cooperation would have been too little and too late. When a surplus is as large and as abrupt as that of the oil producers, it is best that most of it be financed by an extension of credit.

The final point I should like to raise is this, and it is perhaps extremely heretical for an international official. We have to ask ourselves whether the case for deliberate international control over reserve creation has not been weakened by the advent of floating rates. I say this because, under a floating-rate regime, countries should find it relatively easy, with par values, to adjust the average level of their reserves to whatever their national targets may be simply by adjusting their intervention policies. This is certainly true for countries other than the United States, and even for the United States it is true if the United States chooses to intervene in the currencies of other countries.

To be sure, there is a distinction between optimal reserves—optimal from a world standpoint—and nationally desired reserves. Moreover, there is a danger that the United States, under such a system, would be forced back into the sort of passive role, the "nth-country" role, in the international monetary system. There is a danger, too, of confusion and friction from the mutual accumulation of national currency claims. Nevertheless, I think this is a question to which we really must devote some thought, whether the case for deliberate centrally internationally controlled reserve creation is as strong under floating rates as it certainly is under par values.

Professor Shimano shares Professor Triffin's view that it is the asymmetry of the reserve system that has led to the breakdown of the par value system. He says that since the supply of reserves depended on the U.S. balance of payments, the choice was between reserve shortage and U.S. deficits, leading in the end to dollar depreciation. I think he is forgetting that the SDR was established before the great debacle. The dollar could probably have been devalued, without inconvertibility, if the United States had wanted it that way. Conversely, other countries who believed they were acquiring too many reserves could have appreciated without the excuse of dollar inconvertibility. And, as Professor Fellner pointed out, most of the reserve accumulation did take place during the period of virtual, or actual, dollar inconvertibility.

In my view, the par value system came to an end because disequilibria were so magnified by capital flows that they could be handled only by floating. The United States, as a reserve center, could not float. The surplus countries took a long time to make up their minds that it was better to float than to import inflation. Perhaps I might interpolate at this point that as an old "floater," someone who has long believed in floating, I have to admit that what has happened has given me to reflect, to some extent.

As I see it, floating seems to be absolutely inevitable as a way of handling capital flows. On the other hand, its achievement in the matter of adjustment leaves something to be desired. Up to now, the adjustment of exchange rates has done very little other than to offset to some extent differences in relative rates of price inflation. That is, admittedly, a considerable achievement. Where it has not succeeded so far is in bringing about adjustment where losses and gains in real income are required to achieve it. The reason for this may well be that, so far as we can see, money illusion has disappeared in most countries of the world—perhaps not entirely in the United States and in Canada. And if that is the case, the ability of exchange rate adjustment to achieve real adjustment is limited. In other words, it may be that devaluation will only work in achieving real adjustment beyond the short run if it is coupled with other measures to control prices and wages.

I have just seen an analysis of the U.K. devaluation of 1967—by Mr. Artus of the Fund—which comes out with a greater devaluation effect than most of the previous studies on the subject. But all of it seems to be the result of some form of price and wage control, either the income policy which immediately followed the devaluation or control over rents or control over farm prices. The author finds that wage rates, over the longer run, react 100 percent to changes in the cost of living. And that is the truth I think we have to face—the possibility that exchange rates, alone, will not achieve real adjustment.

As my final point I should mention that I do not quite follow Professor Shimano's views on gold. He appears to think that gold ought to be revalued and that when revalued it would enhance reserves, but that it would not become a means of settlement. But, in the first place, if we needed more reserves, there are other and more equitable ways of creating them than by revaluing gold. Secondly, if gold is not used in settlements, what sort of a reserve asset is it? The reserve function cannot be disconnected from the function of settlement. Reserves you cannot use are no good to you. It is true that gold can be sold in limited quantities, on the private market, but that was true before there was any question of revaluing gold.

What is really meant by revaluation? Merely to include gold at a higher price in one's reserve accounts, of course, achieves nothing whatever. The use of gold as security for a loan by Italy was not a happy experiment. In my view, gold is simply a nuisance in the international monetary system. Countries will not give it up and they will not use it either; and the sooner we get rid of it, the better. I cannot, therefore, agree with Professor Shimano when he presents gold as something that would, as it were, help along the nursling SDR. I do not think it is helping the SDR in any way; rather, it is hindering the SDR, because so long as countries think that their reserves are worth more than they were before, they do not want to increase reserves still further by issuing new SDRs.

If gold should cease to be a nuisance, it would only be because countries decided to stabilize its value. And once they decide to stabilize its value, it ceases to be a nuisance, but it becomes a threat to the future of the SDR—first of all, because it achieves an immediate and very substantial increase in reserves; secondly, because, in all probability, it will result in an excess supply of reserves, an excess of production over consumption of gold. Private stocks of gold will be dishoarded, once it is certain what the new price of gold is to be. Certainly there would then be no excuse for issuing SDRs for a long time to come. Moreover, should the situation turn around and the old situation of inadequate reserves reappear, the memory that the last time this happened gold was ultimately revalued would, I think, prevent countries from going wholeheartedly into the business of using the SDR as the central reserve asset.

I must say the gold problem is the most difficult problem in the whole international monetary system, in my opinion. The best thing, I believe, would be to encourage the value of gold to fluctuate. Let the value of gold go up and down on the free market until central banks become convinced that it is not really a suitable reserve asset and are willing to surrender it for SDRs at some price which would have to be negotiated.

PART FOUR

TOWARD STRENGTHENING THE COORDINATION OF WORLD ECONOMIC POLICIES

INTERNATIONAL COORDINATION OF ECONOMIC POLICIES

Egon Sohmen

The title strongly suggests that international coordination of economic policies is desirable. If the alternative is belligerence, nobody will question the desirability of coordination. We all remember that the European Community was originally promoted primarily with the political aim of putting an end to Franco-German enmity. It is difficult to tell whether the peaceful relations between Western European countries at the present time were caused by the climate of permanent negotiations within the Economic Community, or whether causation went the other way, policy coordination being possible because of the peaceful attitudes of nations that have learned the hard way that war does not pay.

Coordination should not, however, become an end in itself. Economists, perhaps more than other people, have a professional obligation to be interested in what is being coordinated, and how. A great many subjects can be coordinated among governments in an infinity of ways. Top-level negotiators are a scarce resource, and the public should not be indifferent to the way they spend their time. Lifetimes can be wasted in coordinating peanuts, and it can almost be argued that this has been the case with the European Community.

Uses and Abuses of Policy Coordination— The Experience of the European Community

The staff as well as the Council of Ministers and civil servants in the member countries working on the problems of the European Community have spent much of their time and energy in the first decade of their existence on two subjects: the common agricultural policy and the attempt at monetary unification. The lopsided emphasis on agricultural policy was primarily the result of the political influence of the cheese, sugar and flour producers in France who were willing to consent to the formation of the Common Market only after they were assured that the promising markets of the other member countries would be their "chasse gardée." A rational explanation for the excessive emphasis on monetary unification is more difficult to find.

Some people have managed to construe a link between monetary unification and agricultural policy, but this is not taken seriously any more. Two popular

119

notions had a strong hold on people's minds: (1) that a unified currency was an essential prerequisite for a truly "common" market, and (2) that the fixing of exchange rates within narrow margins was a necessary first step toward complete currency unification. Many will remember how often spokesmen for the community went on record during the middle 1960s affirming that it was perfectly inconceivable that the currency parities of the member countries could ever be changed again with respect to each other. This is worth remembering to help us avoid similarly misguided and costly efforts in the future.

In this connection, it pays to recall a spirited discussion in the early days of the Common Market on whether a "functionalist" or an "institutionalist" approach to economic integration ought to predominate. The late Wilhelm Röpke, in particular, used to attack the Treaty of Rome as a blueprint for a massive bureaucratic planning endeavor. Even those who do not share Röpke's economic and political philosophy may be persuaded by a simple cost-benefit approach to this issue. In retrospect, the functionalist approach, relying primarily on liberation of the internal community market from tariffs and quotas, has been universally acknowledged as a success. The removal of trade barriers has cost very little in resources—it may even have saved some administrative costs—and has apparently been of considerable benefit to the participating countries.

Quantitative estimates of the welfare gains from free trade in the Common Market have, it is true, come out with extremely low figures. Most economists probably have strong doubts about the estimates, and there are good reasons for these doubts. Yet even if the gains in saving costs should indeed have been minor, efficiency of resource allocation may have been substantially improved by increased competition after the opening of national markets. Tibor Scitovsky in particular has stressed this as perhaps the most important source of efficiency gains.

Now these advantages can all be attributed to the functionalist approach to integration. By comparison, the immense labors spent in the attempt to harmonize classification rules for garlic and similarly important kitchen requisites, or in classifying the sixty-four different ways of creating and allocating international reserves, seem to have borne rather more modest fruits.

There are two important lessons to be learned from the experience of the Common Market, and similar lessons are available elsewhere. First, whenever there is a choice, the preferred organization is one that solves as many allocation problems as possible through self-steering mechanisms rather than through bureaucratic procedures. In plain language, we should choose markets rather than market administrators whenever there is a choice. Second, in decisions that will require discretionary action, it may be advisable to pay attention to the advice of reasonably independent observers who are sufficiently far removed from day-to-day politics and sufficiently far removed from the "organization men." In plain language, we should rely more than we do on the advice of academic economists. In the brief history of the European Community, the warnings of so-called "theorists" have turned out to be overwhelmingly more accurate and reliable than the judgments of most practitioners in charge of official policy.

To some extent, the performance of the European Community bureaucracy and related experience elsewhere is easy to explain. Once they have embarked on a certain course, bureaucracies have their own momentum. Not only do they have their own peculiar "déformation professionelle," but their self-interest may frequently diverge from the general interest of the public. In particular, bureaucratic organizations are often biased toward having more than the optimal level of administrative regulation for the matters under their jurisdiction.

Varieties of International Policy Coordination

It is impossible to say much on concrete policy issues in the short space available, so I will be selective, concentrating on topics of current policy significance. In attempting to set out the different areas in which international policy coordination can take place, it seems useful to adopt an analogy to Richard Musgrave's classification of public finance into an allocation branch, a distribution branch, and a stabilization branch. The possibilities of international coordination in the areas of allocation and distribution are so varied that the best course of action should be to refrain from commenting on them here at all. I will therefore confine myself exclusively to the stabilization branch of international coordination. To state my main conclusion forthwith: it appears that in the past too much energy has been devoted to this particular area.

It is not difficult to diagnose the reason for an excessive emphasis on the coordination of stabilization policies. Until recently, we had a monetary system that made stabilization problems in any one country (at least in any one of the more important countries) an international problem. The most important objective of future monetary arrangements would seem to be making sure that inflation or stagnation problems of any one country no longer become an international issue requiring difficult negotiations with other governments. This does not, of course, mean that friendly advice by international agencies or from one government or central bank to another should be ruled out—quite the contrary. But the actual conduct of stabilization policy should be the responsibility of each individual country. If it is argued that a country is not capable of handling stabilization properly, this might be cause for wondering whether the country is mature enough to be politically independent: it seems strange that we should entrust the life and death of their citizens to the responsibility of the sovereign states, but hesitate to do the same for the regulation of their money supply and the levels of taxation and public spending.

From Dirty Pegging to Dirty Floating

One of the ground rules of the Bretton Woods system was that the activities of the International Monetary Fund should, in the words of Keynes, "not wander from the international terrain," that is, they should not interfere with particular domestic policies of member countries. At the same time, however, a system of truly fixed exchange rates with full currency convertibility imposes a straitjacket on the monetary and fiscal policies of member governments in the system. It is wishful thinking to believe that such a system can be made to operate in a much different way from the gold standard, and individual governments and central banks have been manifestly unwilling to conform to gold standard rules. After World War II, full employment was almost universally accepted as a more important policy objective than permanent exchange rate stability. Inflation rates in different countries could under these conditions not be homogenized to the extent necessary to keep currency parities constant over the long run. Bretton Woods could not be made to work because of this basic contradiction among policy objectives.

Since the Bretton Woods system went down, hardly with flying colors, we have been living in a period of more or less flexible rates among the major currencies, with many small countries aligning themselves to one of the major currencies. A very modest European Community "snake" has survived for the time being, and many Latin American countries continue to tie their currencies to the U.S. dollar. Central banks also intervene in a random pattern to prevent excessive fluctuations of exchange rates.

I have some difficulty understanding why many people choose to describe this state of affairs as "dirty floating," obviously a phrase that is not meant to be complimentary. Many of these who seem to object to the restrained intervention we witness now were previously known as ardent supporters of the defunct Bretton Woods system that forced maximum exchange market intervention on member countries. It seems difficult to reconcile these positions.

From what an innocent bystander can tell about the deliberations of the mighty, a search is now under way for a system that would lay down certain rules to which exchange market intervention ought to conform. I am afraid this is a search for a will-o'-the-wisp. A great many forces are at work in the foreign exchange market at any time; the optimal variety and degree of intervention by a central bank is therefore likely always to be determined more by art than by science, however repulsive this conclusion may appear to the planner (or bureaucrat) who is convinced that there must be hard and fast rules for any official policy decision.

The problem can perhaps best be appreciated by considering an extreme solution. Let us assume that all exchange market intervention were to be performed by an international body (such as the International Monetary Fund) and never by any national monetary authority. The international stabilization agency would then presumably have to follow some general operating rules to protect it from the suspicion that it would interfere unduly in the internal policies of sovereign countries. The movement of exchange rates is, of course, crucially affected by monetary and fiscal policies. What makes things particularly difficult is that not only present policies but also anticipated future policies play a decisive role. Should the international stabilization agency take the possible future policies of all member countries into account in its exchange market interventions? To avoid severe disruptions, it would have no other choice than to do so. The future policies of a country depend decisively on the outcomes of elections and the composition of future governments even between elections. The international stabilization agency would therefore be embroiled in a continuous storm of controversy and accusations that it was playing into the hands of this or that political party.

If such an arrangement were tried, I am quite certain that nobody would want it after a short time. We must, I think, come to the conclusion that there cannot be a "scientific formula" for the optimal course of exchange market intervention, and that exchange market intervention must always be left to the individual countries themselves. In considering all possible candidates, I would expect that most of us would finally settle on central banks as the most appropriate agencies for intervention, just as in the past. Although the Federal Reserve and most other central banks have a habit of alternately overchilling and overheating the economy, it would nevertheless be difficult to find other institutions with the necessary degree of technical knowledge and political independence to be entrusted with decisions affecting the external value of the currency. It may be asked why so many economists seem to be afraid of letting central banks intervene in foreign exchange markets without rigid rules for intervention. This fear stands in marked contrast to the general practice of letting the central banks play the instruments of monetary policy largely "by ear" without exact rules.

The objection to arbitrary intervention without fixed rules comes mostly from the spectre of "beggar-my-neighbor depreciation" that has haunted economic history. This old nightmare, carried over from vague memories of the 1920s and 1930s, seems to be out of tune with the main currents of today's world. There was no indication of an overwhelming desire to devalue while the Bretton Woods system lasted, even by countries desperately in need of devaluation. At this very moment, the United States is going through its worst postwar recession, with an unemployment rate of more than 8 percent. In spite of this, few economists are calling for measures to bring down the rating of the U.S. dollar so as to stimulate recovery. Quite the contrary—concern over an "excessive" depreciation of the dollar is being heard from all sides.

In a framework of flexible rates (with "dirty" floating), the old ghost has only the most tenuous basis for survival. A country can be said to cause artificial depreciation of its currency only when it deliberately and continuously buys foreign currencies on a large scale, thus tending to raise their market rating relative to its own currency. This would become apparent in a prolonged buildup of exchange reserves by its central bank. (As a technical footnote, it may be added that a central bank could camouflage this for some time by limiting this intervention to forward markets.) If reserves do not change appreciably over the medium or longer run, this would indicate that the central bank was not operating against the trend of the market, however fast its currency might be depreciating. Although a substantial and sustained depreciation might come about in the wake of expansionary monetary and fiscal policies, such a development could never be a threat to the economic stability of other countries as long as they were not bound to maintain the stability of exchange rates for their currencies. The exchange rate movement would itself be the main instrument preventing unwanted real adjustments in other countries: it would tend to neutralize an incipient tendency for divergent trends in price levels or interest rates. Nobody would claim, of course, that such a process would always work perfectly or that exchange rate movements would unfailingly reflect instantaneous changes in the major macroeconomic variables in different countries. But whatever ripples were not smoothed in this way could be dealt with by using the standard tools of macroeconomic stabilization policy. Without the straitjacket of artificially pegged parities, governments and central banks may have all the freedom they need to conduct their policies in whatever way they see fit.

Enrich-thy-Neighbor Depreciation

Let us now assume that a country indeed engages in deliberate purchases of other currencies on a large scale in order to cause depreciation of its own currency and thus to bring about an artificial increase of its exports relative to its imports. Such a policy would certainly be one way of increasing employment. But is it legitimate to call this a "beggar-my-neighbor" policy, given the international monetary framework we now have?

It is well known that flexible exchange rates are not a perfect insulator against business cycles abroad. When business expands in one country, causing depreciation of its currency, the implied rise of the depreciating country's exports relative to imports acts as a damping force on the rest of the world. This conclusion holds with increased force if the expansion in the first country is caused by a deliberate depreciation of its currency. But any government in another country that does not want this contraction to happen is, when exchange rates are not constrained by rigid pegging, perfectly free to counteract a contractive tendency arising from this or any other cause by expansionary monetary and fiscal policies of its own. The world will move to a new situation in which the alleged "robber country" has increased export surpluses matched by a steady accumulation of monetary reserves while the rest of the world experiences aggregate import surpluses of the same amount. (We assume, to make matters simple, that voluntary capital movements have not changed in the process. The gist of the argument would not be affected if this were to happen.) Expansionary policies in the rest of the world in response to this development will lead to a further increase in rest-of-the-world imports relative to exports. Other countries are now able to consume and invest more than before, while the "robber country" accumulates monetary reserves.

I need not elaborate on the fact that official exchange reserves usually yield meager interest returns if they pay any at all. In effect, the "robber country" lends scarce resources to the rest of the world at bargain interest rates. Rather than being a "beggar-my-neighbor" policy, the sequence of events brought about by the "villain" turns out to have enriched other countries. The rest of the world would be well advised not to tell the "robber country" that there are other possibilities for preserving full employment.

The conviction that artificial currency depreciation is a "beggar-my-neighbor" policy obviously rests on an invalid analogy derived from the 1930s. The framework in which countries devalued their currencies at that time was one of (adjustably) pegged exchange rates, not one of flexible rates. This makes all the difference in the world, a fact that does not seem to be sufficiently recognized. There is a simple reason why "competitive depreciation" appeared as a menace to other countries during the 1930s. The pegging of one currency at a parity that undervalued it by comparison with what the free market forces would have produced caused a reserve drain on other countries that forced them to adopt deflationary policies (as long as they did not devalue their own currencies in turn) at a time when exactly the opposite would have been called for by domestic business conditions. No such constraints are operative in a framework of flexible rates, even one of "dirty" flexibility.

It is worth pointing out, moreover, that competent business-cycle management would call for expansionary measures (whether by monetary or fiscal means, or by artificial currency depreciation) only in the event of a lapse from full employment. Expansionary policy would then only counteract a tendency toward an incipient disturbance in the opposite direction. Under these circumstances, other countries would not experience a disturbance in the first place.

If alleged beggar-my-neighbor policies turn out to be enrich-my-neighbor policies on closer inspection, it is natural to ask whether the opposite policy—that is, an artificial appreciation—would not turn out to be robbing one's neighbors. The answer would be "yes, for a while, and under the assumption that the rest of the world lets itself be robbed." A country embarking on a policy of artificial appreciation of its currency would sell foreign currencies on a large scale. Its current account would deteriorate while the rest of the world experienced export surpluses of the same magnitude and accumulated reserves of equivalent value. More exactly, other countries would accumulate reserves only as long as they did not either adopt more expansionary policies or sell foreign exchange themselves.

Again, I can see no convincing reason for alarm (nor has anyone else seen it, for that matter, so far as I can tell). Any central bank can sell foreign exchange only as long as it has it. Since any individual country is, by definition, only a part of the whole world, and in most cases a small part, whatever disturbance it can exercise on the rest of the world is likely to be only a minor ripple in an ocean of international liquidity.

From Dirty Floating to Clean Pegging?

The conclusion seems persuasive that the world can easily bear "dirty floating" if governments insist on having it, without any real need for policing according to a new system of universally adopted rules. It is undoubtedly true that exchange rate movements have been greater after the collapse of the Bretton Woods system than what some people may have expected. Before it is concluded that this necessitates an international agreement calling for concerted policing of foreign exchange markets, let us recall the following points:

First, artificial pegging of exchange rates obviously managed to hold the pendulum so far out of its equilibrium position that we should not be surprised if it were to swing around hectically for some time before market participants have a clear idea where the long-run equilibrium—or more exactly, the equilibrium path of exchange rate movements—is located.

Second, the oil crisis is universally recognized to have occasioned the most drastic shift in international payments patterns since the end of World War II. It seems natural that this development and the uncertainty it established for a considerable length of time should have created more disturbance than we are likely to have in the future once everything has adjusted to the pattern of inter-national terms of trade.

Third, anyone who expresses dissatisfaction with the way in which present monetary arrangements have absorbed these shocks should ask himself how any alternative system would have responded. It is often said that flexible rates were the only conceivable system under these crisis conditions, but that we should adopt something else under more "normal" conditions. Apart from admiring the enviable optimism that sees a rosy future without major crises, one is tempted to ask why a system that is almost universally acknowledged to have performed well under crisis conditions is expected to perform worse than others in a more peaceful world. This view must certainly call for a sufficiently exact specification of a "degree of normality" at which flexible rates become the relatively less efficient monetary system. It would be most interesting to see a serious attempt to support such a specification.

Fourth, judging by all available indicators, international trade has not tended to increase more slowly after the Bretton Woods system fell to pieces than it increased before, contrary to the dire predictions of its former sponsors. If trade did not seem to be inhibited even by the large fluctuations of the first few years of flexibility, why is it believed that it would be inhibited by the smaller fluctuations one could expect in less turbulent times?

Fifth, some banks are known to have gotten into trouble as a result of large-scale speculation in foreign exchange. Any foreign exchange trader, if not indeed any properly trained bank employee, knows how a bank can avoid foreign exchange risks. Every bank is perfectly capable of holding down its foreign exchange position to as low a level as it considers prudent. If some banks are expected to violate these rules of prudence to an extent that endangers the safety of their depositors, it is up to the legislators of each country to rewrite official banking legislation accordingly. There is no conceivable reason for attempting to design the international monetary system so as to make it bankruptcy-proof for commercial banks. Such an attempt would be doomed to failure in any case.

There is no convincing reason why international machinery would be needed to force individual countries into a "harmonization" of monetary or fiscal policies. International exchange of ideas among theorists as well as among practitioners of different countries on the relative merits of different policy tools is certainly welcome and is likely to be carried on continuously within the organizations and agencies already in existence. That is about all the international coordination that seems to be called for in the area of macroeconomic policy.

The Recycling Issue

The monetary earthquake caused by the oil crisis of 1973–1974 has led to a flurry of consultations on what steps might be needed at an official level by the principal oil-consuming countries. Limitation of space again enforces restriction to a brief summary of some major points.

First, any large and sustained change in the terms of trade of a country or a group of countries calls for a correspondingly large adjustment in consumption and investment patterns to achieve a reasonable equilibrium in international accounts over the longer run. In that respect, the oil price change is not different from a terms-of-trade change caused by any other development. It stands to reason that a drastic change occurring over a very short time may call for more painful adjustments than a mild and continuous change over a longer period. Exchange rate flexibility may facilitate the adjustment process, but no person in his right mind could possibly believe that adjustment can be avoided under any conceivable monetary system. A claim that the adjustment might be partially avoided can only rest on the belief that the terms-of-trade adjustment prompted by the oil price increase might be reversed again before too long. We are probably well advised not to be overly optimistic.

Second, the need for adjustment is a burden that each country must, in principle, bear individually in proportion to its need for imported oil. Realistically international cooperation can only be expected to ease the temporary burden by spreading adjustment over a longer time. Humanitarian considerations might recommend a more or less permanent restructuring of foreign aid in favor of some very poor countries without oil reserves whose populations were already at the edge of starvation before the oil crisis. There is no possible justification for permanent unilateral transfers between the advanced industrial countries on that count.

Third, it is widely thought that there are some compelling monetary reasons for government initiatives in the "recycling" of funds after the reallocation of payments and (over the longer run) the reallocation of assets prompted by the dramatic rise in the oil price. It has traditionally been the economic function of banks to "recycle" funds from persons, institutions, or geographic areas willing to lend at low interest rates to other persons, institutions or areas that are willing to pay more—in other words, to earn an income by borrowing cheap and lending dear. This would lead one to believe that the basic rules of commercial banking should still hold after a change in the international terms of trade, however drastic. The conclusion seems inevitable that the world's commercial banking system must be able to recycle funds successfully, in whatever amount and direction the market calls for, regardless of the onset of the oil crisis. The intensity and the direction of international money flows may have changed, but banks should still be able, as they have been, to transfer funds from areas of low to areas of high investment opportunity. If some existing banks are unable or unwilling to transact some of this recycling business, this should create profitable opportunities for their competitors. Government activity in this area would not seem to serve any useful purely economic function.

MONETARY DEVELOPMENTS AND ECONOMIC POLICY IN JAPAN

Chiaki Nishiyama

This paper engages in what I should perhaps call "Operation Impossible," a battle, one might say, on three fronts.

First, I wish to assert, in contrast to Professor Sohmen, the need for the closer coordination of economic policies between the United States and Japan, and indeed among the advanced countries at large. Although I share Dr. Sohmen's sentiments about superinternational bureaucracy, I deplore, at the same time, a serious lack of policy coordination between the United States and Japan, a lack evidenced by several events in the last few years. In order to illustrate this point, I will be engaged in what I may regard as a battle on my second front, reporting to you what has been happening in the Japanese economy. Professor Uchida has done this already but the difference between his view and mine is that mine is in many ways a monetarist view, which may of course be criticized as too monistic—too simplistic. My third front is an argument against Professor Sohmen and a defense against Professors Stein and Duesenberry. Indeed, I feel as though I am once again going through the oral examination of a Ph.D. committee.

The sudden crisis in world oil supply and price in October 1973 brought into sharp focus the fact that the contemporary Japanese economy simply could not survive unless Japan were allowed to have free market access to world resource supplies. Of course, in spite of the fact that Japan has had hardly any supply of natural resources, the Japanese economy was doing quite well until not so long ago. In 1955, for example, Japan still relied mainly upon domestic sources for its primary supply of energy. And even fifteen years ago, Japan was dependent on imports for less than half of its energy. Since then, however, through its rapid economic growth, Japan has come to lose its economic independence almost completely, and to find itself in almost total interdependence with the rest of the world.

It is true that almost all the advanced countries in the West today depend on imports for petroleum supply, but in terms of total primary energy supply, their import dependence ratio is still less than 50 percent, on the average, while that of Japan is 85 percent. It is no wonder that Japanese society was jolted by the sudden outbreak of the oil crisis. The immediate reaction of the Japanese people was hysterical—indeed there was almost a panic in the society. The

Japanese economy plunged into a severe inflation. And whatever the immediate cause for the downfall of the Tanaka administration may have been, the great inflation and the associated social turmoil since the end of 1973 were undoubtedly its basic causes. At that time it appeared for a moment that Japan had finally come to the end of the era of conservative administration and the emergence of a new coalition government of the Socialist party and the left wing of the conservatives.

Looking back now, however, we must say that the initial reaction of the Japanese to the oil crisis was (like the reaction of many others) excessive, and that many of the predictions which were made then were too pessimistic.

Let me look first of all at the Japanese inflation. It can be said that the outbreak of the oil crisis was responsible for the emergence of the great inflation in Japan, as well as in many other countries. It is, however, one thing to say this and entirely another to claim that the oil crisis was the cause of inflation. The quadrupling of the price of oil clearly increased the income velocity of money, while the quantity of money was kept stable or at least its rate of change was reduced. Hence, many economists came to assert that it was not money but something else, such as the sudden rise of the price of oil, that caused the tremendous increase in the income velocity of money and, therefore, caused the great inflation.

We must realize that the income velocity of money does change and there is nothing unusual about its changing. Though it behaves in principle procyclically, its behavior generally depends upon the degree of uncertainty in the economy. This is typical of the income velocity of money. The real question is whether nonmonetary factors such as the oil price rise are capable of forcing a change from procyclical behavior. Or is it the case that the procyclical behavior of income velocity was this time either accelerated or mitigated by those nonmonetary factors?

Money is, of course, not everything. It is certainly incapable of eradicating all the disturbances that originate from the real sector of the economy. But money is capable of reinforcing those disturbances and amplifying them. The basic reason why Japan has suffered from a severe inflation since 1973 is that the rate of increase in the money supply has been abnormally high since 1971. This increase was carried out by the monetary authority in spite of our repeated warnings. And the fact is that the Japanese monetary authority not only bought dollars and failed to sterilize them as the Germans did, but also increased the supply of Bank of Japan credit by bringing the annual rate of increase in money supply close to 30 percent in the fourth quarter of 1972. How would it be possible not to have a terrible inflation after the economy had been fed this much money?

It is true that the sudden rise of the price of crude oil not only delayed the turning point in the Japanese inflation but also accelerated the inflation. If there had been no sudden rise in the price of oil, the turning point should have come some time around November 1973, inasmuch as the rate of money supply increase had been lowered by the monetary authority from the vicinity of 30 percent in January 1973 to 16 percent by the end of the year. In other words, the outbreak of the oil crisis accelerated the procyclical upswing of the income velocity of money and widened its amplitude. Had the abrupt rise in oil prices instead come at the psychological moment of the procyclical downswing in the income velocity of money, output as well as the rate of employment might have declined severely, and with them the general level of prices.

Insofar as it was the oil crisis that was the immediate cause for the acceleration of inflation, it could be said that an exogenous factor was responsible. But inflation itself is caused only by money and can be controlled only by money. And I am happy to observe that the Italians, in accordance with this principle, are now apparently able to control their inflation, even though Professor Samuelson has declared that such a single-cause explanation is fallacious. "As we apply the best tools of modern economic analysis to the pattern of available evidence, I believe that no monistic theory can be validly maintained. One is forced, by the facts of experience, into an eclectic position. It is not the case where intellectual indecision or uncertainty leads to a hedged position of eclecticism. It is rather that explanation of the varied pattern of ongoing experience calls for bold combination of causations."

He then refers to the long string of causes, such as balance-of-payments deficits of the United States, wage-push, droughts, floods, strikes, cartel behavior, oil, the general devaluation of currencies, and so forth, and, above all, high-employment or full-employment policy. Even in Japan, in response to a witch-hunt fever among the people, the economists have been busy in enumerating various causes for inflation. It is as if we were being given by those economists a guided tour through a fancy department store, where all varieties of goods are displayed, though without quite being able to decide which one to buy, being instead dazzled if not puzzled.

It is true that there do exist such problems in our economy as full-employment policy, administered prices, monopolies, oligopolies, labor unions, and so forth. And our attempts to solve them are not wrong in themselves. But however successful we may be in removing those exogenous influences on inflation from our economy, we will never succeed in controlling inflation without knowing the endogenous mechanism for its development. It is quite true that if we have had a stomach ulcer, kidney trouble—or, for that matter, cancer—or if we were to be fed bad food, our simple cold might well degenerate into critical pneumonia. But our cold, itself, can never be caused by any of these. Our monopolies or oligopolies may well be the cancer of our economy, and high-priced oil may well be the bad food, but they themselves are never the causes of inflation.

Our question is why, in the face of the enormous inflow of dollars, the Japanese monetary authority continued to increase Bank of Japan credit in the last four months of 1972. It was perhaps because of a preoccupation with the behavior of investment. It was apparent to the Japanese monetary authority that investment, especially in large industries, was a deciding factor in business cycles. But investment did not show any significant increase, and the authority did not seem to care at all how big the rate of increase in the money supply was already. It is true that even by the first quarter of 1973, private equipment investment, which from 1966 had grown at an annual rate of 16 to 18 percent on average, had not recovered from what the Japanese public called the "Nixon Shock." Its annual rate of increase in the first quarter of 1973 was down to 3 percent. The Japanese monetary authority apparently never believed that money per se would directly stimulate output or that sooner or later it would increase investment, unless interest rates were sufficiently lowered for investment to be visibly stimulated.

We must, of course, sympathize with the authority to the extent that the Japanese people's propensity to hold money increased enormously for a while after the "Nixon Shock." If money is really to be regarded as a substitute for information, as I believe it is, the uncertainties created by the sudden announcement of the American new economic policies on August 15, 1971, certainly helped to increase the Japanese people's demand for money. But as the new exchange rate for the yen became clear, a consumption boom began to take place in January 1972, a housing investment boom in March, and an equipment investment boom for medium and small industries in June.

The rate of the private investment as a whole was thus already back to 11.3 percent in the second quarter of 1972. The money supply, for which the rate of increase had by that time reached 24 percent (annual rate), was bound to overheat the economy. And yet there was a cry from the large-industries sector for more money in the midst of the unprecedented abundance of money. Moreover, out of the currency adjustment episode, the Japanese public came to be educated to demand an epoch-making rise in governmental expenditures both for infrastructure investments and for social welfare measures. I must confess that I was one of the economists responsible for this public education. In arguing for floating exchange rates and in effect for the appreciation of the yen, we asserted how much better for the nation's welfare it would be to invest in Japan the labor and resources that had been exported in the form of automobiles, televisions, ships, and whatever, in exchange for paper called the dollar.

In the face of the rapidly accumulating dollar surplus, the Japanese business leaders were convinced of the world competitive supremacy of the Japanese economy—many Americans shared the same sentiment—and failed to realize that the surplus came about because of the price stability maintained from 1965 through 1970, while U.S. inflation accelerated rapidly. During that period, the Japanese monetary authority had kept the rate of money supply increase at the 16 percent level year by year. And what resulted from this was an 11 to 12 percent annual rate of economic growth in real terms and a 3 to 4 percent annual rate of price increase. But the people did not pay attention to this. Instead, they were told that the Japanese people worked too hard and that the Japanese worker should have more holidays with higher pay.

Moreover, the United States kept placing strong pressure on Japan to buy more and be quick about it. And it was just about that time that the Tanaka administration came into power with its ambitious plan for remodeling the Japanese archipelago. The administration proposed to build three across-the-sea bridges at one time and extend both the super-express train network and the express highway network all over Japan. And, in fact, it increased fiscal expenditures by 25 percent by increasing both infrastructure investments and social welfare expenditures. The Japanese went on a spending spree. It was only in this general atmosphere as well as under the pressure of fiscal expenditures that the Japanese monetary authority proceeded to raise the rate of money supply increase to 30 percent in the fourth quarter of 1972, on top of the already excessive stock of money. There was thus established a sufficient condition for the outbreak of severe inflation six months to one year later.

It is correct to assert that the interest rate is an intermediary between the monetary sector and the real sector of the economy. And the people in the banking business may find this is familiar in their own experience—that the liquidity position of the economy as a whole is influenced by the changes of interest structure and that this position in return influences investment and finally the business cycle. Indeed, no central bank will issue new money by dropping currencies from a helicopter: it will issue new money only in exchange for some financial assets, changing interest rates in some way or another.

Nevertheless, interest rates are neither the only intermediary between the money sector and the real sector of the economy, nor even the primary path joining the two sectors. The primary path is far more direct. According to the traditional economic theory, especially in the form of the perfect-competition model, information concerning equilibrium market prices is given and all the units of economic activity are price takers. But how can we be sure that the units of economic activity are capable of ascertaining that information without paying for it? In fact, the more there is genuine competition, the more the efforts of the people are really directed toward finding out the information on equilibrium prices.

In order to discover such information and attain equilibrium prices, the people must unavoidably spend their resources, labor and time, which means they must pay costs. In other words, the information on market equilibrium prices of goods and services is itself not a free good but a typically economic good. And it is this situation that any economy must face and will find difficult to solve when it wishes to advance beyond the barter-production economy and prosper.

It is precisely in this context that money comes into our picture and helps us to solve these difficulties. Money, called "liquidity," is a particular kind of good, the information cost of the market equilibrium price of which is zero; whereas all other goods and services are "illiquid," although their degrees of illiquidity, of course, differ from each other. It is precisely because of this that the people may substitute money for goods they demand, insofar as the marginal costs of the price information for those goods are higher than the marginal returns that can be brought about by investing those costs.

Thanks either to the passage of time, or to the intentional and unintentional collaboration of the people in the social process, the information costs may sooner or later approach zero. At this time the people will substitute goods for money. Putting it in the simplest way, money is a substitute for information. Moreover, it is not only interspatial information for which money substitutes. It is intertemporal information for which money more significantly substitutes. It is, I believe, in the former function that money is ordinarily regarded as a medium of exchange. And it is in the latter function that money is usually regarded as an asset. As an asset, money's most fundamental significance is to be found in its being a production factor.

Money facilitates both production and demand. That is, by being a substitute for information, money facilitates the optimization not only of the production activities of the people but also of their consumption activities as well. It is because of this that there always exists some optimum rate of money supply for a nation's economic activities.

Perhaps it must be emphasized, however, that money is not everything. The rate of money supply increase should not be the sole important policy target. Short-term interest rates are also important insofar as business cycles are interest-elastic. And especially, there exists some optimum level for the long-run level of interest rates. Short-term interest rates should not diverge significantly from this level. But, again, such an optimization of interest rates can be attained only by a steady maintenance of an optimum rate of money supply.

Now, let us go back to the Japanese inflation. As soon as the Japanese monetary authority came to realize that the rate of money supply increase was dangerously high, and especially as soon as the authority came to believe that it would not be accused any longer by my friends in the United States (and others) of engaging in "beggar-thy-neighbor" policy, after it revalued the yen once again at the beginning of 1973, it began to reduce the rate of money supply increase. Since then the Japanese effort to reduce the rate has not been disrupted but only reinforced. The rate, which once shot up from the 16 percent annual rate level to 30 percent in the fourth quarter of 1972, came down to 16 percent again, as I said before, at the end of 1973, and to around 10 percent by September 1974. Thereafter it was kept at that level, until the end of 1974. This means that the Japanese monetary authority was engaged in a tightening policy for twenty-four months.

I do not find any other government that has pursued anti-inflation policy so consistently and continuously as this, at this time, of course. As much as the Japanese monetary authority made a mistake in 1971 and 1972, it has done an excellent job in 1973 and 1974. In view of a most consistent (though admirably gradual) and continuous reduction of the rate of money supply increase, it may be asserted that should the rate of inflation fail to decline, the sun would indeed rise in the West. That is the cold fact that the 100 years monetary history of Japan tells us. And it is thus no wonder that in March 1975, the annual rate of increase of the consumer price index came down to 14 percent, and that of the wholesale price index down to 4.9 percent.

I believe that unless the Japanese monetary authority again engages in an excessively expansive policy, the inflation rate for Japan may well be below 10 percent by the end of 1975. This is still a high rate of price increase and certainly not especially desirable. But I think that the great Japanese inflation has definitely been broken. Of course, this does not exclude the possibility of what Professor Uchida called "bottleneck inflation" in 1976. The slow rate of investment in steel, petro-chemicals, and such in the last two or three years is apparent in the Japanese economy as well as in the American economy.

In any case, in the process of controlling inflation, we came to produce the problem of unemployment, as Professor Uchida reported. The number of Japanese unemployed was almost 1 million as of February 1975. And the labor population, including both the employed and the unemployed who were yet seeking jobs, declined in 1974 for the first time in the postwar history of Japan, and moreover by a quarter million. This means that in addition to the 1 million unemployed, another 1 million or so female workers must have left jobs and returned home to be regarded as housewives. The problem of unemployment is indeed becoming serious in Japan, but the unemployment rate is still less than 2 percent, as Professor Uchida reported.

As the Japanese government resumes stimulative measures, the rate of unemployment will stop increasing. Thanks to the fact that overemployment has been the problem of the Japanese economy, the current unemployment is not yet such a serious problem for Japan as it is for other countries. However, we cannot claim that unemployment will never be a problem for Japan. On the contrary, it is remarkable, first of all, that in spite of the universal life employment system in Japan, the current recession has already come to produce the 1 million unemployed. It is remarkable, secondly, that because of the various restraints, such as the rise of prices of natural resources and energies, environmental problems, and so forth, it is now said—as Professor Uchida noted—that the real growth rate of the Japanese economy, in the coming ten years, will and must be 5 to 6 percent.

The government of Japan is now in fact adjusting its long-run policies, or middle-run policies, for such a rate. Should the trend growth rate in real terms be as low as 5 to 6 percent, and should the relative relationship between the rate of wage increases and the growth rate in the past (and especially in the last year) hold for the coming ten years, it seems that about 3 million people might well have to be unemployed—in other words, that a 3 to 4 percent unemployment rate would become a normal thing for the Japanese economy. If such were really the case, unemployment would indeed be the problem for the future Japan. That is why the spring offensive of the labor unions is now regarded as so important.

It is not only a matter of this year alone, but also and especially of the coming years. After all, insofar as the price of oil is kept high, and insofar as we must engage in the massive transfer of wealth from Japan to the oil-producing countries, a relative reduction of the Japanese living standard is unavoidable.

The Japanese were trying to make a fundamental change from the past trend growth rate of wages and salaries in the spring 1975 negotiation—the growth rate, of course, being taken relative to the growth rate of the economy as a whole. This means Japan is now engaged in what Professor Haberler called radical incomes policy, which aims at recovering the downward flexibility of wages and prices, the latter by means of the revision of the fair trade law reported on by Professor Baba. The Japanese economy might well, indeed, be prepared for the coming of the era of low economic growth.

It will definitely be in such an era and not in one of rapid economic growth that the problem of distribution of both income and wealth will become acute, and social tensions increase. Yet from the political point of view, an interesting phenomenon is now taking place in Japan. All the things mentioned so far, such as the inflation, the reduction of the growth rate, environmental problems, unemployment problems, and so forth, seem to point in only one direction—that is, toward the emergence of a socialist government in Japan. And, indeed, at the end of the Tanaka administration in 1974, it seemed almost a sure thing that, if not immediately, at least eventually a socialist government would come into power in Japan.

All the important municipal governments already had either socialists or Communists at their heads. It was they who had most effectively criticized rapid economic growth, denounced environmental pollution, and asserted the need of a more equitable society. And yet the sudden disruption of economic growth has unexpectedly made it clear that the generous programs of those municipal governments were sustainable only if a rapid economic growth rate was maintained. The opposition parties came to be forced to face squarely not only the problems of spending but also the problems of producing. If those parties succeed in solving these problems, Japan might well observe the birth of a genuinely socialist government.

I, myself, do not much agree with the view that there is no longer anything in the future but an era of low growth rates for Japan. This might well be the case, but I am inclined to hold a more optimistic view. It is true that the efficiency of the equipment investment of Japan has been greatly reduced, since on the average 15 percent of such investments are now for environmental control. Because of the people's utter aversion to pollution, it is now next to impossible to find new Japanese sites for investments in the fields of steel, petro-chemicals, pulp and other such industries. In any case, because of the demands from the producer countries, and because of the increasing transportation costs, Japanese industries may well have to go abroad for processing materials. This amounts to job export.

But insofar as a basic reason for the predicted reduction in the real growth rate of Japan is the price of oil, I cannot see why the Japanese economy will not be able to grow at 8 percent, in real terms, instead of 5 to 6 percent. It is true that Japan's energy resource dependence ratio is incomparably higher than that of the other advanced countries, but this, if I may point it out, means that Japan is destined to be a best buyer for the producer countries. The more we buy from the producer countries, the more we are capable of increasing their incomes. The market is composed of buyers and sellers: I cannot see why the interests of the resource-producing countries would seriously conflict with the interests of Japan.

Besides, however strong an international cartel may be, I cannot believe it will be free from the penetration of market forces forever. As a matter of fact, I even foresee the reemergence of an excess supply of oil at least around the 1980s. It might well be true that Japan would never again experience another sustained period of rapid economic growth at the 11 to 12 percent rate, but Japan might well be able to attain 8 percent growth. Then we would not have serious unemployment problems nor social turmoil.

Now, as soon as the price of oil was quadrupled by the OPEC countries, it appeared that unless Japan significantly reduced the volume of its oil consumption, it would surely create a huge deficit in its international balance of payments. And, yet, because of the way oil is consumed in Japan, its rate of oil consumption was directly connected to its rate of economic growth. Most of Japan's petroleum, approximately 85 percent, was for industrial use. Its economy was to diminish in almost exact proportion to the reduction of its oil imports, by creating huge unemployment and a number of bankruptcies. And that was the thing proposed by Secretary Kissinger.

How to finance its deficit was the most serious problem for Japan. But it is clear now that even here, as Professor Uchida reported yesterday, our initial reaction was too pessimistic. Japan's trade this year may well balance. Japan's trade surplus in the latter half of 1974 of course reflected the belt tightening in its economy during that period. But this must not be interpreted to mean that Japan was engaged in export-drive measures. The rate of inflation for Japan was not only the highest but almost unparalleled among the advanced countries. Japan simply wished to reduce that rate, without considering its exports or anything else, and engage in a gradual and yet consistent effort to control inflation. And in the process of this effort, Japan came to produce a surplus, to our surprise.

But the increase in its exports in the latter half of 1974 did not really imply an improved position in international price competition. Japan has not entirely succeeded in controlling its inflation: it has been successful in reducing its fantastic rate, but not in lowering the general level of prices. The reason that Japan came to increase exports, especially to Mid-Eastern countries, South American countries, and the Communist countries, in the latter half of 1974, is that as domestic demand began to simmer down, Japanese firms found themselves able to meet foreign demands again. Unlike the Germans, they had hardly been able to satisfy foreign demands after the Japanese economy overheated in 1973.

The Japanese economy is so structured that it is still producing on a sufficient scale the kind of goods which the foreign peoples demand. But, insofar as the current international monetary system is a system of floating exchange rates, this structural competitiveness of the Japanese economy does not justify the Japanese accumulation of surplus. Indeed, although the international price competitiveness of the Japanese economy has as yet hardly improved, the exchange rate for the yen already has begun to appreciate, not only because of Japan's increase in trade surplus, but also and especially because of the inflow of foreign capital.

Japan's partial success in controlling inflation coincided with an apparent shift in the strategies of the OPEC countries in their use of the petro-dollar. After having learned how dangerous it was for them to move their petro-dollars around in the short term, they have begun seriously to seek longer-term world investment opportunities. This, I believe, is the fundamental cause for the current rise of the yen. Of course, insofar as the recent inflow of short-term capital was triggered by an interest rate differential, the movement toward the further appreciation of the yen may well be stopped as soon as the Japanese government lowers the discount rate. But I suspect that a vicious cycle toward the appreciation of the yen has begun and may not be easily removed by a reduction of interest rates. As the yen appreciates, the Japanese may well try harder to lower the general level of prices and improve their international competitiveness in all aspects. As the Japanese succeed in doing this, more petro-dollars may well come in.

In fact, the appreciation of the yen is really welcomed by the Japanese, though we cannot afford to jump from the 300-yen-per-dollar rate to the 200-yen-per-dollar rate all at once. But the gradual and yet continuous appreciation of the yen will slow the rate of increase in the prices of imported resources. Besides, it will help the Japanese to invest abroad.

The surge of resource nationalism demonstrated by the OPEC countries which demand the industrialization of their own economies is really not against the Japanese national interest. On the contrary, it could be maintained that it came at a most appropriate time for the future of the Japanese economy. Throughout the postwar period, Japan has built large-scale processing facilities at home and brought back raw materials all the way from abroad. While Japan then did not have sufficient capital to develop overseas resources, it still had a sufficient supply of labor. But now the shortage of labor is going to constitute a restraint on economic activities within Japan.

Japan does not intend to import labor, like the Germans or Swiss, in order to overcome this restraint. Instead, Japan now intends to promote the transfer of capital and technology from our country to low-wage countries in order to import from them labor-intensive products and processed materials. Labor immigration only tends to deprive the less developed countries of the opportunities to develop. As the Japanese economy keeps growing and producing more and more sophisticated goods for export, the quality of its imports from developing countries must also continue to be upgraded. Processing of materials in resource-producing countries—wood fiber to pulp, bauxite to alumina, iron ore to pig iron, petrochemical processing—serves this purpose to the mutual advantage of Japan and those countries.

In any case, the major part of the Japanese foreign investment has always been directed toward complementing Japan's comparative advantage position. This investment has largely been in the kind of industries in which Japan has been losing its comparative advantage. Herein lies the significant difference between Japanese capital export and U.S. capital export. Japan's foreign direct investments tend to increase Japanese exports. Joint ventures have been preferred to wholly owned subsidiaries.

In the economic world, the fact that a country lacks a domestic supply of natural resources does not necessarily imply a disadvantage. On the contrary, it can from time to time be turned into an advantage against competitors in world trade. The Japanese steel industry is a case in point. Precisely because Japan has been free from commitment to domestic resources, it could make efficient decisions on investments in this field.

This does not, of course, imply in any way a lack of willingness on Japan's part to cooperate with the establishment of international recycling mechanisms, such as the IMF oil facility, the Kissinger Fund, or some such. Several people at this conference have eulogized the effectiveness of the floating exchange rate system. I myself have argued the adoption of this system for more than a decade, and would like to defend the system and emphasize that because of it we have tided ourselves over severe difficulties in the international monetary markets resulting from the sudden outbreak of the oil crisis. Nevertheless, it is one thing to say this and another to assert that the floating exchange system would solve every international monetary problem. Indeed, the problem we are facing today is once again that of international liquidity, but this time under the floating exchange rate system.

As much as it is foolish for any nation to dip domestically into recession because of a shortage in monetary supply, it is foolish for the economies of the world to plunge into recession because of the inadequacy of the international liquidity supply. Moreover, the international monetary difficulties from which we are currently suffering are, I believe, temporary in their nature. It is, therefore, desirable for us to establish various channels for smoother recycling of the petro-dollar, though I do not believe Japan will avail itself of such channels.

As to the Tokyo Round, it may be said that insofar as Japan has been one of the originators of the round, it sincerely hopes that it will be promoted by the countries of the world, especially since the United States has finally come around. However, this is undeniably a most inopportune time for this. Insofar as the recession has become worldwide, we may well not be able to accomplish much in our effort to promote the Tokyo Round. Moreover, should we become too aggressive in pushing the Tokyo Round, it might well be counterproductive. I believe that should the Tokyo Round succeed in stopping at least the increase of nontariff barriers, this might well be regarded as a great accomplishment. Of course, we must not forget that the steady liberalization of world trade since 1945, which owes much to the contributions of the General Agreement on Tariffs and Trade (GATT), has played an integral role in promoting the unprecedented growth in production, employment and prosperity all over the world.

Now, having said this much, I should like to raise four or five points. Let me indicate several problem areas which may suggest the necessity of closer cooperation between the United States and Japan, if not among all advanced countries.

The first item is a thing in the past—that is, the enormous increase of the rate of money supply that occurred from 1971 to 1973 in Japan as well as in almost all the other major countries. The rate of increase in money supply, which used to be something like 8 percent on an average among advanced countries, was increased to something like 16 percent. The situation was extremely dangerous, especially in view of the fact that the U.S. economy was at that time under price and wage controls, in the face of this tremendous increase of money supply abroad. The U.S. measures really amounted to an export drive on a tremendous scale. It is remarkable that in spite of the existence of several consultation channels between the United States and Japan, or among the advanced countries, no warning of this U.S. step was apparently given.

The second item is the sudden transition from a fixed exchange rate system to floating exchange rates. It is one thing to authenticate the validity of the floating exchange rates and entirely another to claim that there were no disturbances that occurred from the transition. It was Professor Hayek who once cautioned us economists not to mistake our own views for those of the units of economic activity. A much better preparation for the possible disturbances arising out of this transition should have been made in the United States and other countries.

Of course, the first two items I mentioned are already things of the past. But it seems to me that the United States and Japan, and probably other advanced countries, are now once again facing the problem of money. But it is a problem the nature of which is precisely opposite to its nature in 1973 and perhaps in 1972. The problem was then the problem of excess supply. The new problem might well be that of shortage. We have repeatedly been warned that this is an era of uncertainty. Should such a judgment be correct, with money a substitute for certainty, the rate of increase in money supply, which used to be regarded as optimum, might well be not enough for this year.

The third item is an assertion by the United States that the world should cut its consumption of oil by 3 million barrels a day, Japan's share presumably being something like a half to 1 million barrels. As I mentioned before, the rate of oil consumption is directly related to the performance of the Japanese economy as a whole. The sudden rise in the price of oil, of course, necessitates reducing our consumption of oil, but as much as the high price of oil is damaging to the Japanese economy, we cannot afford to create a depression by our own actions. And this area seems to call for closer coordination between the two countries.

The fourth item is the proposal for an oil floor price. We may see some political necessity for such a scheme. But we must be aware of the danger involved in an attempt to politicize a problem which is really economic in its nature. Besides, I believe that political interests, if they are genuinely political, should have an economic basis.

Finally, I deplore a lack of coordinated efforts to retain at least—if not to expand—a free market in both countries.

COMMENTARY

Herbert Stein

I have no serious disagreement with what either of the speakers has said. Professor Nishiyama asserts his position as a monetarist and I generally believe myself a monetarist except when in the company of monetarists. But Professor Nishiyama leaves room for maneuver in his monetarism—that is, enough other things seem to make a difference so that one does not need to feel constrained by his monetarism, so far as I can see. It is the flag he waves, but he does not follow it slavishly. I agree with him on the need for more cooperation, or consultation, or other closer economic policy-making relations, between the United States and Japan and between the United States and other countries. And if there is a difference between him and Professor Sohmen on that point, I feel myself more in agreement with Professor Nishiyama for reasons which may become clear when I comment on what Professor Sohmen had to say.

I was interested in an early part of Professor Sohmen's paper. He said that there are two important lessons to be learned from the experience of the Common Market, the second of which was, in plain language, to rely more than we do on the advice of academic economists. This seemed to me an exceedingly egocentric lesson to draw from the greatest European experiment in the history of political and economic organization since the time of Julius Caesar. And now that I am an academic economist, I hope it will not be considered self-serving of me to enter some demur about that lesson.

The point Professor Sohmen makes is that the academic economists have been more correct in their forecasts and advice than have the policy makers. My point is that they have this particular advantage as long as they are academic economists. If we rely more on them, they cease to be academic. They would become policy makers and would cease to have this quality of being always right. After all, when the gods gave Cassandra the gift of making infallible forecasts, they also gave her the curse of never being believed, which was, I guess, the price of her infallibility. And I am afraid the academic economists would lose their gift if anyone listened to them.

As Professor Sohmen has himself indicated, while his paper superficially has a strong negative view about coordination, or attempts to coordinate economic policy internationally, this negative view is in fact highly selective. That is, what

Professor Sohmen seems to say is that there is a considerable area of economic policy in which coordination may be useful and probably is. And then there is another area where he thinks coordination may not be useful and that is the area he is going to talk about. This leaves open the question of the proper role of economic coordination.

Particularly, he selects for consideration the area of policy, or of economic relations, where he thinks exchange rate flexibility is the most effective means of coordination. And I have always considered myself a floater, as well as a monetarist, but I do think that some of my floater friends are now in the situation of the young boy who just received a new bicycle as a toy. He wants to use it for everything. He wants to drive it around in the house and get from the bedroom to the kitchen on a bicycle, and so on. You just cannot get him off that bicycle. I think the floaters are so happy that they are floating that they just want to keep bobbing up and down all the time. But that was not what I understood to be the object of the exercise. There is no particular advantage in bobbing up and down— it is just in being free to do so that the advantage was found.

In discussing the possible roles of coordination, in the area of stabilization (which is the area he chooses for discussion) he first dismisses all the cases where countries do find a fixed exchange rate tie to be useful. All those relations between little countries and bigger ones are put aside as being unimportant. But in the international meetings that I used to attend, the demand for coordination of stabilization policies, of anti-inflation policies and anti-recession policies, commonly came from those small countries that found themselves tied to the chariot wheel of some bigger country. They wished to have at least a little voice in what was happening to them. Of course, when I was at these meetings, I was representing one of those bigger countries. It did not seem to me a very reasonable demand then, but it seems to have a somewhat greater significance to me now.

Professor Sohmen also either rejects or leaves outside of the area he wants to discuss those cases in which the exchange rate may not be the best method of adjustment. And the leading case these days is in the secondary recycling problem relating to oil. Now Dr. Fellner explained very clearly how we get into the position where some countries do have an interest in relieving other countries of the need to make an instantaneous adjustment in their balance of payments, through the exchange rate or in some other way. That is, he explained how they come to have an interest in supporting these countries, giving them loans on terms or conditions that might not be commercially available. And then, as a further implication of having done this, the creditor acquires an interest in the behavior of the debtor, which is certainly hard to distinguish from an interest in the coordination of economic policy.

We may say that is not coordination; we may say it is just a debtor-creditor relationship; but I think it is very close to what is involved in the whole business of economic policy coordination. And that, I suppose, is how the IMF got into the business of advising everyone on how to behave himself, on the theory that the IMF represented creditors—or at least because the IMF was most assiduous in the discharge of its responsibility of advising everyone on how he should behave toward countries that were creditors.

Now Professor Sohmen excludes this from the category of cases that he wants to consider, on the ground that it belongs in the distribution department. I suppose he can call it what he likes, but it is certainly relevant to the problem of maintaining stability in the countries that are affected. It does seem to me a little peculiar that Professor Sohmen does not mind "dirty floating" when it is done unilaterally, but seems to think there is something wrong with it, or that we ought to discourage it, among two or more consenting parties.

In his discussion of the stabilization problem he talks about the need for countries to have freedom in the management of their fiscal and monetary policy and the fact that exchange rate flexibility gives them that freedom. But I have observed that one of the staples of international discussions of the coordination of economic policy is the question of the fiscal and monetary mix, the particular combination of means by which a country maintains its stability, given the fact that it has a perfect right and now—with the exchange rate floating—a freedom to maintain stability.

Nevertheless, other countries may be affected by the combination of means that one country uses. And this seems to me a legitimate subject for discussion. Furthermore, it is related to another point. While exchange rate flexibility may insulate some countries from the overall effects of measures taken by one country to maintain its stability, or to achieve whatever it considers an appropriate goal, nevertheless there may be consequences for particular industries or sectors which will be of more than national concern. This would seem to me to be an appropriate subject for discussion.

The idea that exchange rate flexibility frees countries from the transmission of the policy of others, even in its simplest and most economic terms, does not seem to me to be true. I do not think that the rest of the world feels that it is insulated from the effects of our serious recession by the behavior of exchange rates. Our exchange rate has been declining, relative to that of the rest of the world, as a consequence presumably of our declining interest rates. And this, it seems to me, has intensified the effect of our recession on the rest of the world.

I used to believe—I guess I still do—that movements of recession and inflation, and particularly of inflation, are transmitted across the world in a kind of psychological and political way, from which countries are not insulated by the exchange rate adjustment. I think that inflation is a political phenomenon, the consequence of political attitudes. An attitude of tolerance toward inflation, an attitude of accepting inflation as a normal way of life, has swept across the world.

Probably we would all find it easier to operate anti-inflationary policies internally if we could take some joint resolution in that direction.

In any case, aside from the area of stabilization, there are, as Professor Sohmen has recognized, numerous possible opportunities—and possible needs—for coordination of economic policy. I think the energy situation is the most dramatic and impressive recent example. I must say I am a little surprised by and I do not know that I understand what Professor Sohmen is saying about the price of oil, or the price of energy, when—having written such an all-out free-market paper—he suddenly discovers that something needs to be done about the price of oil because oil will run out in 500 years.

I found that puzzling. What does he think the price of oil is going to be 500 years from now, so that discounted at 10 percent from then to now, oil is worth more than $10 a barrel? In any case, of course, as Professor Nishiyama said, money is not everything and oil is not everything either, and there are other ways to keep warm.

Supposing that we agree that there are a certain number of areas in which we need coordination, I would raise two questions.

First, can we have coordination—is it possible, looking at the international scene and the kinds of international machinery we have? I think that is the problem, rather than the one which seems to worry Professor Sohmen, which is the spectre of an international bureaucracy taking over. I think that the international bureaucracy is irritating, but it is not yet in the position to take over the making of any major decisions. In fact I think that the problem is that we are likely to get less coordination, or cooperation, or consultation, than we need, rather than too much, just because of the natural tendency of all governments to pay attention to what is closest at hand and best represented in their political process in the shortest run. Those tend to be the local interests. To be concerned with international coordination means to give more weight to other interests than those. So it seems to me the natural tendency is to have too little, rather than too much, international coordination. And I think it is easy to be very negative about the possibility of getting coordination—or cooperation, or whatever.

For the purposes of the OECD, in 1969 and 1970, when Paul McCracken used to go to those meetings, he invented the term "concertation" of policy to get away from the implications of coordination, which seemed to suggest that some international czar was going to tell us what to do. There is a whole family of words which imply different degrees of intensity of joint action. But I think that—whatever we call it—as one looks at our experience, he must say that the market operates here, as well as in other places, and when there is a strong case for it, we do tend to generate coordination or consultation.

I think the energy situation is a good example of this. I think that the International Energy Agency and the agreements connected with that have gone

146

farther than one would have expected a year ago. And I think this happened because at least some of the participants felt strongly moved and believed that there was a considerable common interest. I think the whole establishment of secondary facilities for financing, in connection with the oil problem, is another example of the possibilities of doing something when there is a very great interest in doing it.

Once when I was at an OECD meeting I noticed that in the headquarters they had a list of the meetings that are being held, and there was a meeting being held on the international coordination of standards for automobile headlights. I thought to myself that this was a very trivial thing, compared with what we were discussing, but that was a subject on which they would probably reach a decision, whereas we would not. It was important to someone that these headlights should be coordinated, whereas international coordination of what we were talking about was not important to anyone. As in everything else, so here, we will not get what we do not believe we need.

The second question that concerns me is whether the United States government is capable of participating in any kind of coordinating, or concerting, or consulting, with other countries. First we must get ourselves coordinated. Are we at present in a position to discuss important economic matters with other countries and arrive at some decisions? There are several problems here, of course. For one thing, by the time the U.S. government goes to meet with other countries, it has arrived at a U.S. government policy. This policy has been fought out so hard among various government agencies, it represents such a hard-reached compromise, that the United States is in no position to move away from it, once it gets at the meeting, because if it did move, several agencies would fall off the bandwagon.

The second problem, of course, is that once the administration has discussed something, has arrived at something, we still have the U.S. Congress to contend with, a Congress that has not been represented and may not go along. I think this is particularly difficult on the setting of macroeconomic policy. I can see that the Treasury, the Council of Economic Advisers, the Office of Management and Budget, and the Federal Reserve will have all agreed that our policy is to have a $52 billion deficit. And I can see the possibility that we will then have gone to an international meeting and have concerted our policy, and have all agreed that that is the U.S. policy. But how do we implement it? How do we keep the deficit from being $100 billion? We have certain handicaps. I certainly think that is a problem that needs to be worked at—of course not only in its international aspects. But I think we ought to be seeing what we can make of this area of international coordination. We need not think there is a danger of too much international coordination.

James S. Duesenberry

I found both papers interesting and I should be happy to go a couple of rounds on monetarism, sometime, but I do not believe this is the day for it, so I will try to deal mainly with issues raised by Professor Sohmen's paper.

I felt the passage of time when I was reading that paper. When I was a young man like Professor Sohmen, I believed that my famous predecessor in the Harvard Money and Banking chair, John Williams, was making an easy living, because whatever anybody said, he replied, "It's more complicated than that." And now I find that this applies to Professor Sohmen's paper. In fact, that is what I have to say: "It's more complicated than that." I want to deal here with two of the issues he raised. First, the recycling question and, second, some problems about more general stabilization policy.

We had some talk at this symposium about whether we should be looking at the mountain or at something else, and questions have been raised about the Euro-currency markets. What those questions are really saying is that there may be a volcano inside that mountain. And I think there may be.

If I understood Professor Sohmen's observations on the petro-dollar problem, he was saying that there should be some configuration of exchange rates, interest rates, in different countries that would give each country a position on trading accounts consistent with the flows the country is receiving from OPEC long-term investment and OPEC liquid-assets investment. There is some set of exchange rates and interest rates that should make this position balance out for any given set of tastes on the part of the OPEC countries as to what kind of investments they want to make. And presumably the aggregate must induce them to invest enough to balance off the aggregate oil trade surplus, the difference between what the OPEC countries receive from the sale of oil and what they spend for current account goods and services.

There are two problems that I think arise there. One I will allude to briefly. Professor Sohmen said this will involve some shifts in the terms of trade, which may be hard on some countries, because they may find that the amount of exchange rate adjustment they have to make in order to maintain their balance-of-payments position will involve a considerable deterioration in their terms of trade. That is certainly true. I think we are remarkably lucky that thus far no country has concluded that there are other means to adjust the trade balance besides exchange rate changes and that some of those other ways might involve less deterioration in terms of trade.

After all, various kinds of trade barriers could be raised, which, at least in the short run, a country might think would permit it to improve its trade balance position without major deterioration in terms of trade, since the country could be selective about which relative prices it reduced or increased. Thus far we have not had much of that. I think it might turn out that, if some countries find it

148

difficult to cover their oil deficits without major deterioration in their terms of trade, they may resort to special measures and we may find that these special measures will produce a net loss for the rest of us. This may be an incentive for some type of coordination to make that resort unnecessary.

The second problem is one connected with the Euro-dollar market. At present—and with our present arrangements I suppose we must expect it to be the case for some time in the future—a substantial part of the liquid assets being acquired by the OPEC countries is going through the Euro-currency markets. In effect, the OPEC countries are acquiring, through their surplus, a Euro-dollar account with some European bank, or branch of a U.S. bank, which gives them a dollar-denominated claim. That bank, in turn, may be prepared to lend the dollar-denominated claim to an Italian firm, or a French firm, or any firm willing to pay the rate. Eventually, there will be a conversion into the local currency and the dollars will have been recycled through that system.

In effect, those banks are operating as intermediaries, as Professor Sohmen said. They are borrowing from the OPEC countries at one rate, and they are finding some borrower to whom they can lend at a sufficiently higher rate to make it worthwhile to take the risk. So they are intermediaries, just like intermediaries anyplace else, as Professor Sohmen said. What has happened here, though, is that a few banks in this operation are now increasing the scale of their intermediation very rapidly.

Some of these banks have a European home base, some of them have a Japanese home base, and a good many of them are branches of U.S. banks. Now one might hope that they all know exactly what they are doing, that they will all have sufficient capital, maintain sufficient liquidity, so that any mistakes they make will be simply absorbed by their own stockholders. But I think we should not be entirely sanguine about this. I think we have problems where the supervision lies and where the responsibility lies. What would happen if a branch of a U.S. bank were to fail? Which monetary authority would have the responsibility to deal with that situation?

This is a rather difficult problem. Certainly it is not in the ordinary realm of U.S. banking situations. On the other hand, the U.S. banking authorities would have to face the fact—if the bank that failed were a branch of a major U.S. bank, even though it were a separate subsidiary—that whatever happens to the branch will affect the credit standing of the holding company and the American-based bank. That bank could prove to have 30 percent of its liabilities in federal funds and certificates of deposit, which could run out like water in a tub. You will remember that Franklin National lost $400 million in one day.

We have our contingent liability if one of the banks in this business should get itself into any serious trouble (and I think there are many scenarios which could produce the trouble) so that the situation could have fairly substantial repercussions. If it did not involve any financial difficulties in the United States, that would only be because the U.S. authorities, in the end, agreed to absorb some of the loss, or at least take part of the risk while they were finding out what the loss ultimately was going to be.

This means that it is not a fair proposition to say we have commercial banks out there and they take in this money, and they lend it out, and if they make a mistake, that will be too bad for their stockholders, but nobody else is involved. In fact, it is probably going to turn out that the United States is already holding an insurance contract which it never signed: it is, in fact, involved in the risk. Presumably the financial authorities of some other countries would be similarly involved.

It seems to me that in these circumstances there might be some case for international coordination and at least for discussion of the ways in which the risks involved in very large amounts of international short-term lending, in the rapid increases in the amount of lending, should be shared among the countries. Of course it may be that in the end the stockholders will take most of any losses that may occur. But it seems to me that this is a fairly substantial risk consideration, something we ought to be thinking about and something on which there is a need for some international arrangement.

Let me turn to the second point, the more general stabilization question. Here I want to look at Professor Sohmen's point that if we have flexible exchange rates, any country can have whatever monetary and fiscal policy it wants, without having balance-of-payments problems. Now it is certainly true that with greater flexibility in exchange rates, there is less need for large reserves and less constraint on domestic policy from fear that one will lose one's reserves and wind up in a balance-of-payments crisis; or from fear that one country will have to soak up funds from another country, thereby affecting one's own domestic money supply. But I think there are some limits to this.

I think that first of all there is a problem of adjustment on the part of the domestic trading interests in a country to the implications of the overall stabilization of the balance-of-payments position. When the exchange rate has to move in order to keep the system in balance, this means a change in the competitive position of some traders. And this may arise from non-trading reasons. For example, if interest rates move, causing a change in the flows of capital, one can expect the trading account to make the corresponding adjustment. And on a long-run basis, that expectation is reasonable. The countries which have considerable capital and relatively low interest rates presumably ought to be countries which have a low interest rate inducing the export of financial capital and an exchange rate permitting them to export a corresponding amount of real capital.

I think this is true in the long run and it is a great improvement over the situation we had in the early 1960s, when our interest rates were lower than

European ones, but we could not establish an exchange rate which permitted us to get sufficient exports of physical capital to cover that financial capital. But while I think it is true in the long run, the cyclical swings may create quite a lot of trouble for total reliance on the exchange rate mechanism. If you have short-run cyclical swings which are not in phase for the different countries, and if at the same time there are lags in the response to changes in exchange rates, lags which are of different length from the lags in response to interest rates, there can be a fair amount of trouble. Perhaps it would not be earth-shaking trouble, but it should be worth considering.

I think some of the tales that Professor Nishiyama was telling go with this. If you imagine the United States in a slump which calls for low interest rates, and the slump moves the interest rates down leading to a balance-of-payments deficit, then—until exchange rates have changed—you can see that other countries will be faced with one of two alternatives. Either they keep their exchange rates the same, in which case they collect dollars, and—depending on the nature of their financial system—may find their own money supply influenced in a way they do not want, or to avoid that, they let their rate appreciate, which ultimately changes their trading position.

They may actually find themselves getting it both ways. First, the appreciation may not have any sales effect; they will keep on acquiring the dollars anyway, pumping up their domestic supply. And just about the time they receive the effects of that, they begin to discover that their trading position is deteriorating from the earlier changes in the exchange rate. I think that when we get away from steady-state economics to the economics of fluctuations, with different time phasing in the fluctuations, we run into problems. How many of those problems can be solved by international coordination I am not sure.

It seems to me that there could be some understanding of the terms on which a country will soak up a balance-of-payments surplus when it appears that the surplus results from some cyclical configuration, and of the terms on which the country will unwind that position. Without going so far as to say we must have an elaborate set of rules of the game of exchange rate adjustment, I think some understanding of what everyone is doing, and some discussion of whether there are circumstances in which it would turn out that everyone would be better off if they were doing something else, is at least worth trying.

It seems to me this is a significant problem, even though our experience with trying to get people to change the mix of their policies has not been particularly encouraging. It does not seem to me that flexible exchange rates have made that problem go away entirely: there is still a good deal of it left. Maybe it is now reduced to a size which might be soluble, whereas the old problem would not be soluble. In any case, these are the complications that I see in Professor Sohmen's accounts.

DATE DUE

MP 728